The ABC Movie
of the Week
Companion

This is a TV Tidbits book.

Other books in the series include:

Barnabas & Company: The Cast of the Classic TV Series Dark Shadows, by Craig Hamrick

Big Lou: The Life and Career of Actor Louis Edmonds, by Craig Hamrick

The TV Tidbits Classic Television Trivia Quiz Book, by Craig Hamrick

Funny Ladies: Sitcom Queens, by Michael Karol

The Lucille Ball Quiz Book, by Michael Karol

The Comic DNA of Lucille Ball: Interpreting the Icon, by Michael Karol

The TV Tidbits Classic Television Book of Lists, by Michael Karol

Other books by Michael Karol:

Lucy A to Z: The Lucille Ball Encyclopedia

Lucy in Print

Kiss Me, Kill Me

Sleeps Well With Others

For more information, visit www.sitcomboy.com.

The ABC Movie of the Week Companion

A Loving Tribute to the Classic Series

Michael Karol

iUniverse, Inc.
New York   Bloomington

iUniverse, Inc.

New York   Bloomington

The ABC Movie of the Week Companion
A Loving Tribute to the Classic Series

iUniverse books may be ordered through booksellers or by contacting:

iUniverse
1663 Liberty Drive
Bloomington, IN 47403
www.iuniverse.com
1-800-Authors (1-800-288-4677)

Front and back cover design by Michael Karol
Front cover still from *Trilogy of Terror* courtesy of Jim Pierson and Dan Curtis Productions

ISBN-13: 978-1-60528-023-3 (pbk)
ISBN-13: 978-0-595-61661-9 (ebk)
ISBN-10: 1-60528-023-2 (pbk)
ISBN-10: 0-595-61661-5 (ebk)

Printed in the United States of America

iUniverse Rev. date 10/24/08

To Mom, who nurtured my love of the movies.

And to all those obsessed enough to know what a Zuni fetish doll is…

The length of a film should be directly related to the endurance of the human bladder.

—Alfred Hitchcock

Contents

Acknowledgements

Special thanks to the very gracious Denise Nickerson and David Hedison, for sharing their MOTW memories; to my late friend and editor Craig Hamrick ... you still inspire me; to Jim Pierson of Dan Curtis Productions for his invaluable help with the *Trilogy of Terror* pics, especially the cover photo; my copy editor, Joe Diliberto; Saul Fischer; Robert Gutowski; Billy Ingram of the fabulous Web site TV Party (see the Bibliography); Ron and Howard at Photofest; and The New York Public Library for the Performing Arts, at Lincoln Center.

Foreword by Denise Nickerson

I'd done a lot of television work by the time I appeared in *The Man Who Could Talk to Kids*. And I'd also done some theatrical-release movies. This was a fun combination of the two: It wasn't as stressful as a traditional movie set, but the atmosphere was very professional and I was treated like a little "movie star."

The ABC Movie of the Week series was, I believe, groundbreaking. Before this series, a lot of movie stars would never have even considered appearing on television. But these made-for-TV films had such good production values, good directors, and crews that they drew talented casts.

Like a lot of people back then, I loved watching the MOTWs, and I was thrilled when asked to be part of one of them. *The Man Who Could Talk to Kids* was my first job after moving to California. I had known co-star Scott Jacoby (who played the troubled lead character) for years when we both lived in New York. As a matter of fact, I had a crush on him. We filmed it at a beach north of Malibu; I think it was Point Mugu in the Santa Monica Mountains; it's got everything from mountains to sandy beaches and dunes.

Anyway, there was a nude beach on the other side of this one huge rock. I didn't see any wandering nudists, but it was the talk of the crew! I also recall that I had a scene in the film where I had to crush a butterfly with my bare hand. I agonized over that for weeks before filming, and then I think it ended up on the cutting-room floor. I'm almost certain my role was that of another patient of (teen counselor) Peter Boyle's (who was very nice to me during filming). I believe the whole thing with the butterfly was to teach me how to let go of things; evidently, my character had issues with that.

Robert Reed—who co-starred with me in this movie, as Scott's father, and on an episode of *The Brady Bunch* I did the next year—was nice, polite but distant. I had already met Brady mom Florence Henderson about six years earlier. My best friend lived in her New York apartment building, and sometimes we would hang out with her daughter, Barbara. So it was fun re-connecting with her. The only Brady kid on the show I really had contact/scenes with was Peter (Christopher Knight), and he was just great. The episode was called "Two Petes in a Pod." Unfortunately, I played the homely girl, one of the two he had dates with. They put large horn-rimmed glasses on me, flipped my hair like Sandra Dee—I wasn't looking my best, that's for sure! But, I digress…

I really enjoyed being part of a MOTW—just like I know you'll enjoy reading this book. Michael is a gifted writer with whom I got a chance to spend some time when we were both guests at the Big Apple Comic and Nostalgia Convention in 2005. (We bonded over our mutual love of Lucille Ball.) It's obvious that he has a genuine fondness for the MOTWs, and if you love them as much as he does, you'll have a great time walking down TV memory lane with him.

—Denise Nickerson

Denver

Child star Denise Nickerson is best remembered for her turn as Violet in the original Willy Wonka & the Chocolate Factory *(1971). Prior to that film, she had appeared for two years on the cult soap* Dark Shadows. *Denise subsequently made appearances on TV (*The Brady Bunch, *1974) and in films (*Smile, *1975) through 1978, at which point she left acting.*

List of Abbreviations

Key
An asterisk (*) before a movie title indicates the film was a pilot for a projected TV series
MOTW = Movie of the Week
MOTWs = Movies of the Week

Introduction to the 2nd Edition

Movies resonate in the same way that songs, books, and television shows do, a very special way: Often, a scene or a plot twist or a pivotal character will stay with you, long beyond the first time you viewed it, and become a touchstone in your memory. You can remember exactly where you were and what you were doing when you first saw the movie.

Few series have become cultural touchstones in the way that *The ABC Movie of the Week* has. Its lengthy run and ambitious goal (to present an original film every week to a demanding audience, one that was much larger than the typical audience of today) were partly the reason, but primarily it's because these short films—most running about 77 minutes to fill a 90-minute time slot—were funny, sad, real, horrific, and yes, cheesy. Memorably so.

These movies ran when I was in high school (through the spring of 1971) and then college. As a teenager growing into a young adult, it's safe to say that many of the topics and ideas I saw on *The ABC Movie of the Week* were relatively new to my mindset. I had grown up a closeted gay kid in a small town; having heard only the negative about being a homosexual, imagine what it was like to see *That Certain Summer* as a sophomore in college, just as I was getting ready to spread my wings.

Like many kids of the era, I was familiar with drug use. The tortured heroine of *Go Ask Alice* spoke to me, and helped convinced me not to go too far off the deep end. *The ABC*

Movie of the Week was a like a good friend, one who made me laugh when I needed it, and one who occasionally presented some sobering issues that needed a public platform but rarely got one. Sure, there were pure escapist films, too, and those that really don't merit any further consideration (you won't find lengthy reviews of those here; with more than 240 films to review, I had to focus by necessity on my favorites in the series).

But it's a rare prime-time series that bats a thousand year in and year out. *The ABC Movie of the Week*'s record was better than most.

When I came up with the idea for this book in early 2004, I knew there would be a few other fans of *The ABC Movie of the Week*, but I never reckoned on the power of baby boomer nostalgia. With very minor publicity and no marketing, this little book took off on its own and late in 2007 was designated an iUniverse best seller: the company made it a Star title.

That meant a redo, and the majority of reviews have been added to or updated. In many cases, I added excerpts from interviews with MOTW stars. There's another important difference: this edition has pictures, and the welcome participation of Jim Pierson of Dan Curtis Productions. He supplied the cover photo, a still shot—a frame from the actual film—of the Zuni fetish doll from *Trilogy of Terror*, one of the best-remembered films of the series; the back cover shot of a screaming Karen Black; and more, including his support of the project. I cannot thank him enough.

I found several films that eluded me the first time around, although one ardent fan assured me that, with one exception, the dates for missing movies in the Appendix (see page 181) were exactly right, because he had kept his own detailed TV diary of the entire era (now *that's* a couch potato!); turns out those were in fact dates when the *Movie of the Week* was preempted, repeated, or replaced with other programming. I've noted which films or programming ran on every one of the formerly "missing" dates.

I've added more trivia to entries where possible (for example, the many big-screen clones of the Cloris Leachman thriller, *Dying Room Only*), and rewritten some of the text, but kept it all in the spirit of my original goal: to fondly salute (and sometimes tweak) these films that obviously left a strong imprint in the memories of many.

In the first edition, there was a separate chapter on those MOTWs that were pilots for projected series. In this edition, all films have been placed in their proper season and pilots are marked with an asterisk (*). Film (pilot) sequels are listed under the original title. And, of course, there are now pictures included to help jog your memories even further.

So, once again, here we go: It's the late 1960s. The counterculture is in full swing, and you're getting ready to be entertained by a new viewing choice: the movie made specifically for television.

—Michael Karol
New York
October 2008

The ABC Movie of the Week:
A Brief History

It started not with a bang but with traditional PR bluster. On June 24, 1969, ABC released a story to the press headlined "25 Original 90-minute Movies Made Especially for ABC-TV Comprise the Most Costly Series in Network History." That was quite a mouthful. But ABC had no idea how influential its series of movies would become for many viewers, especially those of the baby boomer generation.

Barry Diller, then ABC vice president of feature films and development, said at the time, "What we are trying to do is broaden the base of familiar television anthologies and movies-for-television. First, the 90-minute form provides us with the opportunity to do justice to that special echelon of story ideas, which don't quite work in the standard one- and two-hour television program forms.

"Second, unlike previous movies-for-television packages, *Movie of the Week* is drawing its films from several production companies. And [we're] coupling the individual movie to the company best equipped to produce it. This…takes into account not only the production company's experience with certain story formats, but also its ability to enlist the talents of the most appropriate producers, writers, and performing talent."

For example: Thomas-Spelling productions (as in, Danny Thomas and Aaron Spelling), referred to as "a leader in suspenseful, compelling drama," has "put its stamp on *The Ballad of Andy Crocker*, a powerful film about a returning Vietnam soldier. And Screen Gems, long identified with the making of outstanding comedy films, is turning its creative energies to such light-hearted pictures as *In Name Only* and *Gidget Grows Up*."

(Spelling later partnered with former ABC head of programming Leonard Goldberg, who helped develop the movie-of-the-week format. Spelling-Goldberg produced some of the most successful movies and TV series of the late 20th century, including *Brian's Song, Charlie's Angels, Fantasy Island, Family, T.J. Hooker*, and *Hart to Hart*.)

Diller went on (for two pages) to note that the MOTW was "an excellent opportunity to further expand the scope of network television," by filming stories that could not be done in a weekly series due to their "fixed costs and linear story formats." Extensive research was used to determine what viewers wanted to see; considering the era, it was likely done in Focus Groups. And of course, ABC had been closely watching its network competitors.

According to Billy Ingram of the Web site TVParty. com, "In October, 1964, the first full-length film produced especially for home delivery debuted, called *See How They Run*, starring John Forsythe." The Museum of Broadcast Communications in Chicago adds, "…The historical turn came in 1966 when NBC contracted with MCA's Universal studios to create a regular series of world premiere movies-made-for-television. The initial entry of this continuing effort was *Fame Is the Name of the Game*, inauspiciously presented on a Saturday night in November 1966." *Fame Is the Name of the Game*—starring Tony Franciosa as an investigative reporter for *People* magazine (way before *People Weekly* debuted)—was the first such pilot to earn a regular series slot on the network. In *The Name of the Game*, Franciosa shared the star position with Robert Stack (a crusading crime magazine editor) and Gene Barry (head of the publications empire) in rotating 90-minute mystery, action, or thriller movies. Susan Saint James won an Emmy for her work as Barry's spunky editorial assistant. It ran for three years, from 1968–'71.

Ingram notes, "Watching the success NBC was having with its TV-movie specials, ABC's Barry Diller realized the time was right to update the old anthology format, but with a twist. He scheduled a weekly series of original movies for fall 1969, with shorter running times (90 minutes) and strict budgetary restraints to make the productions commercially viable."

Due to the limited budgets ($400,000 to $450,000 each), "Universal declined to partner with ABC for Diller's folly," Ingram reports. "Lean and hungry independent producers like Aaron Spelling, Quinn-Martin and David Wolper eagerly jumped in, resulting in a more raw-edged product than the blander Universal telefilms."

In an era before cable TV became the standard, when there were only three networks to watch, period, plus a PBS station and occasional UHF (usually local) programming in larger cities, ABC was gambling a bit. The concept would no doubt be astronomically price-prohibitive today.

But even as Diller was proposing this risk, there was a large pool of fine actors from many backgrounds who were willing to tackle unusual subject matter—this was the 1960s, let's not forget—and go a bit further than the normal half-hour or even hour drama format would allow. There was also a large resource of talent in those actors and actresses who had been Golden Age movie stars or character actors: by the late 1960s the old studio star system had changed so much they were no longer welcome on the big screen, except perhaps as someone's parents or—god forbid, for the female stars at least—a rising star's *grand*parents.

The television audience was not so picky, already used to seeing big stars on the small screen. And on TV, a star's long history made them welcome in the public's living rooms. So it's no surprise the MOTW became a haven for female stars of, shall we say, a certain age. (And for that reason, some movie buffs affectionately refer to the MOTW as "employment parties.")

Consider the odds against producing *any* kind of quality television. The fact that more often than not a provocative, funny, sad, terrifying, or even socially responsible film was produced for broadcast (I know it's network TV we're talking about, but it was true), twice a week, is nothing short of amazing.

And keep in mind that Diller and ABC had an ace up their sleeves: Many of the MOTWs were pilots for projected series that would conceivably air on ABC. So in one sense, the MOTW functioned as an in-house "pilot factory" for the alphabet net. And a profitable one—since most failed pilots are never broadcast, they can't earn back their cost through sponsorship. Not so the weekly ABC movies.

Production values in all areas were top-notch. The opening logo for *The ABC Movie of the Week* series featured an instrumental piece by Burt Bacharach, then one of pop music's top composers, titled "Nikki," a love song to his daughter. Sample lyrics (which were added later and fortunately never heard on the show): "Nikki, it's you. Nikki, where can you be? It's you, no one but you for me." The music, without lyrics—only a few, dramatic bars of "Nikki" were used—served as the perfect appetizer to the movie when paired with the opening graphics, a sequence that heralded the use of computer graphics that would be the norm in coming years.

Film historian Jeff Vilencia told TVParty.com, "That opening is one of the very first examples of computer-style animation; it's actually shot with a device that utilizes a series of mirrors. That animation system (called slit-scan) is still in use. I saw a recent IMAX film that used it—it was very cool! It kinda looked like that old *ABC Movie of the Week* logo." Another famous use of this effect can be seen in the climax of *2001: A Space Odyssey*.

Diller's press release was issued the summer before the series debuted, and by then 13 of the 25 films for the first season had been filmed. Less than five months later, on November 4, 1969, the MOTWs had become so successful that ABC announced it was renewing the series. The 1970–'71 season would offer 26 films. Martin Starger, then vice president in charge of programming for ABC, noted that the budget for the series would grow from the first season's $15 million to $16.5 million, allowing the MOTW to remain the (then) most expensive series in television history. In May, 1970 Starger told *Variety* the budget was actually $18 million.

Diller added that there could be "special situations" in the second season warranting films that ran for two hours or more.

When the MOTW series was renewed for its third season (1971–'72), ABC estimated the movies were reaching "nearly 14 million homes on the average minute" during broadcast. That represented a 10 percent increase over the comparable period a year earlier. Perhaps that's why ABC stepped up production and added a 90-minute movie slot on Saturday nights in the fall of 1971, called *The ABC Movie of the Weekend* (which disappeared for a year and came back as *The ABC Suspense Movie* in the 1973–'74 season). Also running from 8:30 to 10:00 p.m., these MOTWs indicate that the alphabet network was running two per week before its official schedule added the Wednesday night MOTW in 1972–'73.

All the Saturday movie titles are present in ABC's two-page 1974 ad celebrating the filming of the series' 200th film, indicating they were officially part of the MOTW series. On several occasions, MOTWs ran on Wednesdays (before the *Wednesday Movie of the Week* debuted) instead of Saturdays. Perhaps ABC was testing the timeslot. And in the final seasons, MOTWs occasionally ran on Saturday nights as well as Tuesdays and Wednesdays.

TV Guide noted, in its Oct. 28, 1972 issue editorial, "With the continuing clamor of complaints about the quality of television entertainment, you may not have noticed a trend that points toward significant improvement. The trend is to diversity—exemplified by the growth of TV-movies and miniseries…. After a ragged start, the tailored-for-television features have gotten better and more consistent. Certainly not all are first-rate, but a *Brian's Song* or a *My Sweet Charlie* [not part of the MOTW series] is a big improvement over three ordinary episodes of three ordinary sitcoms." The MOTW was here to stay.

In the fall of 1974, the series' final season, ABC could be forgiven the hyperbole of its trade ad text: "When we started the *Movie of the Week* in 1969, it was a bold experiment destined to become the most successful original feature film series in television. Today, it is recognized as an entertainment form and an art form that has earned a permanent place in television programming, and has earned for us the name: The Movie Makers."

ABC was celebrating the 200th MOTW: a slice of sadism called *The California Kid*. It was a typical late-in-the-series flick, which ran on September 25, 1974 (see Season Six for details).

The MOTW had, indeed, been a groundbreaking series that would continue to exert its influence on programming for years to come. But the writing was on the wall. The success of the MOTWs had ignited network TV's favorite strategy: Imitate anything that gets good ratings. Imitate it *a lot*.

When the 1975–'76 season began, *The ABC Movie of the Week* was gone from the schedule. By then, there were movies airing on TV almost every night, sometimes more than one a night, some of them made for TV, some not. This was pre-cable, so the viewing public actually *wanted* to see movies on network television. The *ABC Sunday Night Movie* had been a staple for the network since 1964 and it also added a *Monday Night* and *Friday Night Movie*. These were joined by the *NBC Sunday Mystery Movie* rotation (*Columbo*, *McCloud*, and the like), *The NBC Monday Night Movie* and *NBC Saturday Night at the Movies*; as well as the *CBS Thursday Night Movie*.

The following season, NBC tried an hour-and-a-half *Movie of the Week* on Wednesday night, which lasted for one season. In the 1977–'78 season, CBS offered the *CBS Wednesday Movie*; added a *CBS Tuesday Movie* in 1979–'80; and kept movies on those two nights variously through the 1990s. The Tuesday movie was more regularly on the network's schedule.

Meanwhile, *NBC Saturday Night at the Movies*, which was the first program to put feature films in prime time TV, and debuted in the 1961–'62 season, breathed its last after the 1977–'78 season. ABC still runs a Sunday night movie on occasion as special programming in a two- or three-hour time slot.

But the movies themselves are the reason *The ABC Movie of the Week* is so fondly remembered. Alternately touching and mawkish, scary and funny, sophisticated and cheesy, their plots and characters, and the wonderful actors who portrayed them, still resonate in the minds of viewers who made the MOTW a Top 10 show for several seasons and a cultural touchstone to this day.

The Ratings Race

Note: The *Tuesday Movie of the Week* aired from 1969-'75. The *Wednesday MOTW* aired from 1972-'75.

Ratings:
1969–'70
—Number 22, 20.9 share (12,226,500 viewers)

1970–'71
—Number 6, 25.1 share (15,085,100 viewers)

1971–'72
—Number 5, 25.6 share (15,897,600 viewers)

1972–'73
—Tuesday MOTW: Number 17, 21.5 share (13,932,000 viewers)
—Wednesday MOTW: tied at Number 25, 19.9 share (12,895,200 viewers)

1973–'74

—Tuesday Movie: Number 21, 21.0 share (13,902,000 viewers)

—Wednesday movie: not in the Top 30, though *The ABC Sunday Movie* (which showed original and Hollywood flicks, and had debuted in the 1964 season) was Number 24 with a 20.7 share. ABC also had a *Monday Night Movie* this season (Number 26 for the year, 13,372,400 viewers) ... not to mention the made-for-TV movies on the other networks. Overkill was beginning to set in.

1974–'75

—Neither movie made the Top 30; the series was canceled at the end of the season. But the movie-of-the-week concept continues to thrive.

Of Salaries and Stars

An April 8, 1970, article in *Variety* noted that though stars were in less demand for feature films due to a slowdown in production, no such problem existed in TV land. "Top guest-star price next season will be Aaron Spelling Productions' *Movie of the Week* shows for ABC-TV, where the ceiling is usually $15,000, although on occasion as much as $20,000 has been paid," the trade paper noted.

The top guest-star salaries for other production companies like Paramount was $7,500, the same as Universal's pay for a stint on its revolving mystery-movie series, *The Name of the Game*. By contrast, a role on a top long-form drama like *The Virginian* (a 90-minute Western) was $4,000. Variety shows also topped out at $7,500 for guest stars (think *Rowan & Martin's Laugh-In*, *The Dean Martin Show*, *The Flip Wilson Show*, and *The Carol Burnett Show*). Nice work if you could get it.

A word must also be said about the career-nurturing effects of the MOTW on stars of all ages and types, from classic Hollywood divas to newly minted ingénues. Once the MOTW became a success, every star, wannabe, and has-been wanted to be in one. The MOTWs were successful at showcasing all kinds of actors:

• Those possessing old-fashioned star glamour (Bette Davis, Olivia de Havilland, Fred MacMurray, Melvin Douglas, Myrna Loy, Ray Milland, Vera Miles, Helen Hayes, Ann Sothern, and Barbara Stanwyck all performed in MOTWs, several in more than one)

• Stars-to-be (Jeff Bridges, Burt Reynolds, Nick Nolte, Sally Field)

• Stars who, by appearing in MOTWs, kept their careers alive and ultimately resurfaced bigger than ever (William Windom, who found his long-running groove on *Murder, She Wrote*; Leslie Nielsen, who emerged as an unparalleled, and unexpected, comedian in *Airplane* and *The Naked Gun* films)

• New stars who were fated to either make it or disappear from view for a variety of reasons (Peter Duel, Kim Darby, Lynda Day George, Ben Murphy, Stefanie Powers, Martin Sheen, and Sissy Spacek)

And then there were others, who, as with any time period in Hollywood, you just have to shake your head in wonder and ask, "Why?" (This group includes Yvette Mimieux and Ken Berry.)

Season One: 1969–1970

The MOTW logo used a mechanical technique of animation called slit-scan, featuring constantly shifting text and graphics that enabled the designer to create a psychedelic stew of design and color, foreshadowing our current use of computer graphics. Imagine the words "The Movie of the Week" coming toward you as the lines featuring "World Premiere" headed toward the center, getting smaller and more blurry as they disappear at a mid-point horizon line, similar to the text that opened the Star Wars films … and you'll get an idea. Re-creation by Michael Karol and Ronald White

About Pilots and Sequels: Many of the most memorable MOTWs were pilots for television series, which met with varying degrees of success. All films that were made as pilots are marked with an asterisk (*) in the regular MOTW season listings. Some of the films were given a second try as a MOTW sequel to the original, and the most popular ones got a third chance to go to series. All are listed and reviewed together in the regular listings, under the season and date on which the first movie aired. Those that went on to become TV series are noted within the review text. [Note: The popular ABC comedy anthology series *Love, American Style*—which ran from 1969-'74—began life as a MOTW, but was never broadcast as a movie. It was sold as a TV series before that could happen.]

Seven in Darkness, September 23, 1969
Ad tag: "A plane crash traps seven blind people in the wildness. Eight top stars."
The debut MOTW served up a plot Hollywood has rehashed time and again, to varying degrees of success: A plane crashes in a remote area of the world, and the survivors must band together to make it back to civilization alive. The twist here is that all the survivors of this flight are blind, and they're fighting their way down a rugged mountain. This flick is remembered for Milton Berle's non-comic performance. *The Charleston* (West Virginia) *Gazette* reviewed the movie thusly on September 22, 1969: "ABC's new series of 90-minute movies made for TV begins with a highly melodramatic tale. Although its plane-crash-survivor theme is familiar, the fact that all the survivors are blind people on their way to a convention adds an interesting gimmick to the film. Their efforts crossing dangerous mountain terrain is [sic] visually suspenseful, and the on-location production is first-

rate. Taking a cue from past films of this genre, the survivors are mostly well-played stereotypes—Milton Berle as a gruff businessman not resigned to his blindness, Sean Garrison as the ex-Marine with a secret about an incident in Vietnam, Barry Nelson as a jealous group leader, Lesley Ann Warren as an over-protected blind folk singer, and Dina Merrill as a woman blind from birth." Popular supporting character actor Arthur O'Connell portrayed a lonely widower and *The Flying Nun*'s Alejandro Rey was also featured. Based on the 1963 book *Against Heaven's Hand*, by Leonard Bishop.

• Besides being the first movie of the week to air, this was Berle's first TV-movie, as well as Paramount's.

• Garrison did a lot of TV work in the 1960s and 1970s, and specialized in playing military men.

* *The Immortal*, September 30, 1969

The MOTW was quick to jump into all its genres, including science fiction. In this one, a race-car driver (Christopher George as Ben Richards) discovers a distinctive component in his blood might make him immortal. Alas, a greedy, rich old doctor (Ralph Bellamy) wants George's blood for himself. With the always-watchable Jessica Walter and the luscious Carol Lynley, three years before donning hot pants and surviving *The Poseidon Adventure*. This served as the pilot for a short-lived series (15 episodes in 1970-'71) starring George and Lynley. The greedy, rich old doctor of the MOTW became a ... greedy old millionaire who followed George (via a hired mercenary) and had him brought to his estate for periodic transfusions. The weekly series chronicled the adventures of George and the people he met each week, kind of like a sci-fi *Fugitive*.

• Walter, best known as a dramatic actress (she went on to play the deranged stalker of 1971's *Play Misty for Me*) eventually displayed previously unknown comedy chops as the venomous mom in the hilarious sitcom *Arrested Development* (2003-'06).

• The series was rerun the following summer, but at least one paper complained of the lack of original hot-weather programming, claiming the networks were being even stingier than ever. Noted the *Oil City* (Pennsylvania) *Derrick* on May 8, 1971, "ABC is replacing its canceled *Young Lawyers* with reruns of *The Immortal*, which bombed earlier this season and was canceled before New Year's as a regular series. Chris George starred as a man with a rare blood factor, which would keep him alive forever under all circumstances except wily enemies who wanted excess transfusions. Or something like that."

* ***The Over-the-Hill Gang***, October 7, 1969
* ***The Over-the-Hill Gang Rides Again***, November 17, 1970
Pat O'Brien is the retired Texas Ranger who sees corruption in his daughter's town while visiting, and gets three of his old pals (emphasis on the *old*: Walter Brennan, Chill Wills, and Edgar Buchanan) to help clean up the place. Kristen Nelson portrays his daughter, and (then) real-life mate Ricky Nelson (in keeping with the *Ozzie & Harriet* tradition) portays her husband. Adding comedic spice are Gypsy Rose Lee (in her first TV movie and final film appearance), Andy Devine, Jack Elam, and Edward Andrews. This pleasant and occasionally raucous comedy from Thomas/Spelling Productions spawned a second MOTW pilot, with Fred Astaire (following his TV role in *It Takes a Thief*) replacing Pat O'Brien. Look for Western clichés galore in the sequel, including the white-garbed hero vs. the black-hatted villain. Before shooting of the first film began, Joan Quarm of the El Paso, Texas, *Herald Post*, wrote in her February 1, 1969 TV column, "I met Edgar Buchanan and found him … sporting a stubble beard for his

next film. He spoke of the sense of humor necessary to stay in the business, and the team spirit developed on a show such as *Petticoat Junction*. He likes feature film work for its greater acting challenge, and is enthusiastic about the *The Over-the-Hill Gang*, which starts shooting on March 11. In it he plays one of a former gang of rough-riding shooting cowboys, who leaves the old folks' home to answer a call from its leader and clean up a town. As he told it, the plot is a gem."

• Ricky (later Rick) Nelson was in between singing careers when he appeared in the original *Over-the-Hill Gang*. He'd just weathered being a teen idol, but was still several years away from success in the country-rock arena.

Wake Me When the War Is Over, October 14, 1969

You see, Ken Berry accidentally falls out of a plane in Germany just as World War II is ending, and is found by a lovely baroness (Eva Gabor) who takes him in, and likes him so much she doesn't tell him the war has ended. This comedy has a dream classic TV sitcom cast, including Jim Backus *(I Married Joan, Gilligan's Island)*, curmudgeonly Parley Baer (almost 200 TV series guest roles over 45 years, from *I Love Lucy* to *Star Trek: Voyager*), Alan Hewitt (the suspicious Detective Brennan on *My Favorite Martian*), and everyone's favorite German, Werner Klemperer *(Hogan's Heroes)*.

* *The Monk*, October 21, 1969

No, it's not about fun in the abbey, it was a pilot vehicle for the breezy charm of George Maharis, starring as private dick Gus Monk. Janet Leigh, Carl Betz *(The Donna Reed Show)*, Jack Soo, Jack Albertson, Raymond St. Jacques, and Joe Besser (one of The Three Stooges for several years in the 1950s) do their best to enliven this effort. Described by the *Pasadena* (California) *Star-News* on September 7, 1969, as, "a fast-paced story of intrigue and organized crime.... Filmed in San Francisco, the story unfolds against the colorful backgrounds of the Golden Gate Bridge, Chinatown, and Fisherman's Wharf." It depends on whether you're a fan of Maharis' easy-to-take personality. In an interview with the *The Odessa* (Texas) *American* on November 1, 1969, a few weeks after the show aired, Joan Crosby wrote, "When George Maharis was introduced to Gustavus Monk three years ago, Maharis didn't like Monk because he was 'slick, glib, uninvolved.' When Maharis played Monk recently on an ABC-TV movie of the week, the character had evolved into what George calls 'a handyman of life, a guy who does what he thinks, who is a broken-field runner, who cares.' There is a possibility, if reception to the film is good, that Maharis and *Monk* may return to the home screens on a regular basis, possibly next January. However, George isn't making any quick decision, since there is also a possibility of his starring in a Broadway musical, slated to begin rehearsing next December." [*The Monk* never made it to series, and as far as I can determine, Maharis never made it Broadway.]

After Maharis left his hit show *Route 66*, which ran for four years (1960-'64) and earned him an Emmy nomination, Maharis "hinted he and TV were through forever." By 1969, he was ready to make amends: "Honest George," Crosby noted, "admits that not all his films [have been] good and that TV isn't really *all* that bad. The tiff is over. 'I've been offered TV series every season since I left,' he says. 'There was one offer to go into an established hit, but I didn't see what I could bring to it. But I have always said I would do another TV series—if it was right.'" Maharis never got another long-term series role, either, though he was very active in TV through the early 1980s, last appearing on the small screen in 1990.

* ***The Young Lawyers***, October 28, 1969

This is my first "actors-you-never-thought-you'd-see-in-the-same-flick" rundown: Georg Stanford Brown (soon to be a *Rookie*); Zalman King as Aaron Silverman; sturdy character actor George Macready (*Gilda*; TV's *Peyton Place*); African-American ingénue Judy Pace; James Shigeta; Keenan Wynn; and Richard Pryor! The plot is so late-sixties liberal as to be clichéd nowadays: Older established lawyer uses hungry young newbies to help poor and similarly needy people who can't afford it. Only King and Pace made it to the TV series, along with newly cast Lee J. Cobb as their boss. The series, beginning in September 1970, lasted for one 24-episode season.

• King is perhaps better known for his post-acting career as the producer and writer of the Cinemax-style soft-porn classics *9½ Weeks* and *The Red Shoe Diaries*.

The Pigeon, November 4, 1969

Sammy Davis Jr. (yes, "The Candy Man" himself) stars as a hip private eye on the trail of a missing girl who doesn't want to be found. With Dorothy Malone, Pat Boone, Patsy Kelly, and Ricardo Montalban. The MOTW casting directors sure knew how to come up with eclectic ensembles, to say the least. A press release described the movie as "a story of mystery and humor" with Davis as "a private investigator who takes on Dorothy Malone and her daughter, Victoria Vetri as clients when they are harried by a 'syndicate' leader, played by Ricardo Montalban. A bit of off-beat casting has singer Pat Boone playing Sammy's duplicitous partner."

• Vetri's exotic looks served her well as Miss September 1967; in 1968 she was chosen Playmate of the Year.

* **Spy Killer**, November 11, 1969
* **Foreign Exchange**, January 13, 1970
Smith. John Smith. Television already had its James Bond parody (*Get Smart!*), but this MOTW and its sequel cast sexy starlet Jill St. John as Mary Harper, the fashion model/girlfriend of Smith (Robert Horton of *Wagon Train*), a former spy, now private eye, whose ex-boss, Sebastian Cabot (*Family Affair*), manipulates him into coming back to work as a secret agent. St. John returned to play Mary Harper opposite Horton one more time. In the second MOTW, Mary is kidnapped and Smith must retrieve her. The Russians are involved, and so, once again, is Sebastian Cabot, calling the shots as Smith's boss, Max.
• St. John must have used her "top-secret" experience in these MOTWs to bag the role of Tiffany Case in 1971's 007 caper, *Diamonds Are Forever*. She became the first American Bond girl.
• Writer Jimmy Sangster made his name in horror and suspense flicks, first as an assistant director, then as a writer, including an episode of the TV series based on the MOTW *The Night Stalker*. He also wrote season five MOTWs *Scream, Pretty Peggy* and *Maneater*.

* **The Ballad of Andy Crocker** (a.k.a. **Corporal Crocker**), November 18, 1969
The unusual team of Lee Majors (as Andy Crocker) and Joey Heatherton (Lisa) play out the sadly still-topical (as of this writing) scenario of a returning Vietnam vet (Majors) who finds life isn't quite as he left it; his childhood sweetheart (Heatherton) is married to someone else, for one thing, and former business partner Jimmy Dean (a.k.a. the singer and sausage king) has betrayed him. Another time-capsule cast rewards the lucky viewer: R&B crooners Marvin Gaye and Bobby Hatfield (one

of the Righteous Brothers) appear as Crocker's Army buddy and business associate, respectively; *Bewitched's* Agnes Moorehead as Heatherton's mom; Pat Hingle as Crocker's dad; and Jill Haworth and Peter Haskell play "hippies." The *Florence* (South Carolina) *Morning News* review (of a repeat performance on May 30, 1970) was positive: "The returning Vietnam serviceman faces problems that are uniquely his—problems of adjustment, of change, and of status. Such concerns form the theme of *The Ballad of Andy Crocker*," and the paper called Majors' work "a touching portrait of a returning soldier who finds himself bewildered by a world he never made." This Thomas/Spelling pilot never sold.

In Name Only, November 25, 1969

A crack comedy cast (including Michael Callan, Eve Arden, Ruth Buzzi, Bill Daily, Elinor Donahue, Herb Edelman, Paul Ford, and Elsa Lanchester) lifts this film. "Relationship consultants" Callan and Ann Prentiss learn that some of the marriages they arranged aren't legal. But will the affected couples want to tie the knot for real? Not enough people wanted to know; this Screen Gems pilot never made it to series. *The Anniston* (Alabama) *Star* reviewed the film the night it aired, calling *In Name Only* "easily the best comedy presentation *The Movie of the Week* has offered since its debut [which, it must be pointed out, was a mere two months earlier]. Ann Prentiss and Michael Callan star as a pair of marriage brokers who are shocked to discover a minister they have hired is really an actor with no powers for tying the well-known knot. He has already married three of their couples, all of whom must be re-wed, if their business is going to survive. Problem seems to be with the couples, all different … and that doesn't bode well for the brokers. The couples are: Bill Daily and Elinor Donahue, Christopher Connelly and Heather Young, and Herb Edelman and Ruth Buzzi."

• A loose remake of 1952's *We're Not Married!*, which also starred Eve Arden.

• Prentiss is comic actress Paula Prentiss' look-alike sister.

• Young is better known for her starring role in the sci-fi series *Land of the Giants*.

• Callan, a popular light comedian of the time, had recently starred as Peter Christopher in a short-lived but well-remembered sitcom called *Occasional Wife* (1966-'67), about a fake marriage, to friend and upstairs neighbor Greta (Patricia Harty). Peter believes being "married" will help him move forward faster in his job. Callan and Harty really were married for a short time, after meeting on the series.

Three's a Crowd, December 2, 1969

This cute comedy takes the oft-used plot of a man, in this case an airline pilot, juggling two wives in different cities. Larry Hagman portrays the charming bigamist. Jessica Walter and E.J. Peaker are his two very different wives. With Harvey Korman, *Will & Grace*'s Shelley Morrison (then co-starring on *The Flying Nun*), and Norman Fell giving an early audition for *Three's Company* as a lecherous elevator operator who knows the truth. Future *Charlie's Angel* Farrah Fawcett has a small role as a hitchhiker. Hal Erikson of the online *All Movie Guide* was not fond of this flick: "For some reason, the made-for-TV *Three's a Crowd* was rerun to death in the early 1970s. Perhaps it's because local TV station managers couldn't get … the 1940 theatrical features *My Favorite Wife* or *Too Many Husbands*, the plotlines of which are strikingly similar to *Three's a Crowd*. Larry Hagman plays a pilot who disappears and is presumed dead by his wife. Seven years later, however, Hagman pops up in another city, married to someone else. Jessica Walter and E. J. Peaker co-star as the pilot's two brides. The film's title tune was written by Bobby Hart and Tommy Boyce, the same team responsible for several of the Monkees' 1960s hits."

• ABC shot a TV pilot of the same name, with the same plot, for the 1967–'68 TV season. Starring Bill Bixby, it never sold.

• Bob Pickett, better known as Bobby "Boris" Pickett, who had a monster hit with "The Monster Mash" (as of this writing, the only song ever to hit Billboard's Top 100 on three separate occasions), had a bit role in this movie.

Daughter of the Mind, December 9, 1969

This one is notable for its sinister atmosphere and supernatural plot, presaging the current (as of this writing) interest in all things super-normal, as evidenced by the popularity of dramas like *Supernatural* and *Ghost Whisperer*, and "reality" shows like *Ghost Hunters* (which debuted in 2004 and spun off *Ghost Hunters: International* in 2008). A cybernetics professor (and how many of *those* were there in 1969?!) played by Ray Milland claims his daughter is trying to get in touch with him. Big problem: She's deceased. The plot thickens when the government becomes involved, along with a professor of parapsychology. The supporting cast includes Don Murray, Gene Tierney, Edward Asner, and popular sixties/seventies teen actress Pamelyn Ferdin as the daughter in question. The ending is not quite what it should have been, but I remember getting the shivers when first watching it.

• Bob Gutowski, who writes the "DVD Savant" column for the website DVDTalk.com, begs to differ: "Pam Ferdin, *popular*? 'Ubiquitous' is more like it! From sitcoms to commercials, to supplying the voice of Lucy in several of the animated Peanuts specials, this kid was everywhere." Ferdin, born in 1959, was a busy young star, appearing in nearly 70 television shows (*Bewitched*, *Star Trek*, *The Andy Griffith Show*), voicing cartoons (*Sealab 2020*, *It's a Short Summer, Charlie Brown*, *The Cat in the Hat*), was a series regular (*The Paul Lynde Show*), and did TV movies and films (*The Beguiled*, *Charlotte's Web*) between 1964 and 1974. She was blonde, often pigtailed, and had a clear, strong voice that indicated beyond-her-years maturity.

The Silent Gun, December 16, 1969

Lloyd Bridges is a stoic sheriff of a rowdy Western town who has vowed not to use his gun after almost killing a child. So he uses an empty gun and his wits to outdo the bad guys. Also starring Ed Begley, Edd Byrnes, and Pernell Roberts, the *San Antonio* (Texas) *Express* noted in its TV listings that, "The silent gun belongs to Bridges, playing a feared gunslinger who unloads his weapon for keeps after nearly killing an innocent child. Resolved to rely solely on his reputation, he gets his test when he finds himself in a position to upset the balance of power between the good and bad guys in a frontier town. Okay, but it would have been better as a three-minute antiviolence commercial."

• Bridges starred in a *Studio One* presentation of *The Silent Gun* in 1956, along with newcomer Anthony Perkins (who'd make his mark in 1960's *Psycho*).

Honeymoon with a Stranger, December 23, 1969

This thriller has Janet Leigh losing her new husband during a honeymoon in Spain. Friendly police captain Rossano Brazzi helps her look for him, and they discover his past is littered with ex-wives he ran out on. When hubby finally is found, Leigh insists he's an imposter. No one believes her, of course. Horror cult icon Barbara Steele is Leigh's sister-in-law. *The New York Post* called this "a fun and a fast 90 minutes" with "an ingenious and surprise" solution. Such a good story it was remade twice during the MOTW series: see *And No One Could Save Her*, February 21, 1973, and *Dying Room Only*, September 18, 1973.

* ***Gidget Grows Up***, December 30, 1969
* ***Gidget Gets Married***, January 4, 1972

Yes … Gidget grows up and becomes Karen Valentine, then someone else. The appealing Valentine (*Room 222*) is the main reason the first movie works, and she is helped by a top-notch supporting cast, including Paul Petersen (*The Donna Reed Show*) as Moondoggie, Bob Cummings as her understanding dad, and Paul Lynde as, well, Paul Lynde. Gidget returns from several years in Europe as an exchange student, but finds her love life is as complicated as ever. As for *Gidget Gets Married*, the title says it all. Monie Ellis and Michael Burns (unknowns who remained unknowns) played Gidget and Moondoggie; support from Don Ameche, Lynde, Joan Bennett, and Elinor Donahue couldn't lift this silliness above an average grade for a sitcom. As a movie, it gets an F.

• After Sandra Dee originated the title role of *Gidget* in the 1959 hit, the part was played by Deborah Walley in *Gidget Goes Hawaiian* (1961) and Cindy Carol in *Gidget Goes to Rome* (1963). James Darren played faithful Moondoggie in all three films. On TV, Sally Field started her career playing the perky teen in a fondly remembered 1965 sitcom that ran for a year.

• Both these MOTWs were pilots for proposed series that didn't sell, though the character finally found a second TV home as a syndicated series, updated for the 1980s (*The New Gidget*) and ran for two seasons, 1986–'88, with Caryn Richman in the title role.

Black Water Gold, January 6, 1970
Keir Dullea, Bradford Dillman, France Nuyen, Lana Wood (Natalie's little sis), and Ricardo Montalban are all after the sunken treasure from a Spanish galleon. One's a scuba bum, one's a marine archeologist, and one's a Mexican historian. This MOTW pre-dated the disco-era *The Deep* by seven years, but the plot keeps coming back to haunt us, with different actors.

Carter's Army, January 27, 1970
They couldn't make a Vietnamese war film for TV about racial insensitivity in 1970, but it was safe to set it during the "good" war that happened several decades before. An all-star cast adds fuel to this earnest "message" flick about a tough, bigoted captain (Stephen Boyd) placed in charge of a black squadron during World War II. If you're thinking "blaxploitation for TV," you're almost right, but the cast (including Richard Pryor being serious, Glynn Turman, Rosie Grier, Moses Gunn, Robert Hooks, and the always-smooth Billy Dee Williams), makes it worth a watch. The *San Antonio Light* had this to say: "Interesting World War II drama benefits greatly from the fine performance of Robert Hooks as the lieutenant in charge of an outfit of black soldiers. Stephen Boyd plays a white southern officer who clashes with Hooks and his men, while trying to carry out a dangerous mission involving a strategic bridge marked for demolition by the Nazis." Sixties ingénue Susan Oliver plays a German double-agent who helps the men out.

Along Came a Spider, February 3, 1970
Suzanne Pleshette stars as the spunky widow of a murdered scientist who tries to find out whodunnit by disguising herself and cozying up to his former colleagues. That alone is enough to get me to watch, but in addition to the delightful Pleshette,

the plot is intricately spun. *Peyton Place*'s Ed Nelson is the prime suspect. The *Delaware County* (Pa.) *Daily Times* liked it: "*Along Came A Spider* is a complex mystery drama that should keep you close to your set. A widow is convinced that her husband was killed by a fellow scientist to gain his secrets. To prove it, she changes identity, plans an affair with the man and succeeds in assuring herself of his guilt. [Try *that*, Jessica Fletcher!] Then she concocts a murder plot, with her new self the victim, and the scientist, the murderer. After it all works to perfection, with the widow returned to her own identity and the scientist convicted of murder, things begin happening to prove that he had been innocent all along."

The Challenge, February 10, 1970

This forgotten Cold War-era gem pits two men (hardened mercenary Darren McGavin and cunning warrior Mako, from an unnamed Communist Asian country) against each other on a deserted island in a fight to the death, to claim an object that fell into the sea. They do this instead of having the countries fight a full-out war. Clever, eh? But both sides do their best to stack the odds against the other.

• Directed by George McCowan, who helmed many MOTWs and here took the pseudonym Alan Smithee; directors put that name on a movie with which they don't want to be associated. Directors as diverse as Don Siegel (*Death of a Gunfighter*), Michael Ritchie (*Student Bodies*), and Dennis Hopper (*Catchfire*) have used the Smithee alias.

Quarantined, February 24, 1970

"There's a good deal to commend *Quarantined* ... despite a script that smacks of the daytime medico serials," reported *The Capital Times* of Madison, Wisconsin. "Fiction is blended with real-life drama, in the form of a kidney transplant being performed on a tempermental Hollywood star. The real films come from the UCLA Medical Center while the fictional patient is lovely Sharon Farrell, who gives an excellent performance. The donor is played by Wally Cox as an adoring fan [named Wilbur Mott], in the best *Mister Peepers* style. The premise of the production however, is a clinic run by the family who founded it, and the personal and professional problems inherent in its operation. These are complicated by the actress, and another patient who collapses in the waiting room, showing definite signs of a contagious disease." Frankly, they had me at Wally Cox, whom I remember fondly as a regular on *The Hollywood Squares* from the mid-1960s until his death in 1973.

• *Mister Peepers* was Cox's sitcom (1952-'55), in which he played mild-mannered but good-natured junior high school science teacher Robinson Peepers, and was forever typecast.

Mister Jerico, March 3, 1970

The Avengers' debonair Patrick Macnee finds himself in familiar territory in this failed pilot, but on the other side of the law, as a jewel thief after a big diamond. This caper leans toward the comedic with Herbert Lom (*The Pink Panther* series) as his nemesis, Afro'ed Jewish comedian Marty Allen as his partner, and scrumptious Connie Stevens as Lom's secretary (and Macnee's helpmate). As the *Abilene* (Texas) *Reporter News* noted when the flick was rerun during the summer, *Jerico* starred Macnee "as a charming con man. But keep your eye on co-star Connie Stevens." The *San Antonio Express* reviewed the movie the night it aired: "Macnee … is just as debonair as he was as Mr. Steed in *The Avengers*, but he's a notorious swindler. Jerico and his inept partner, played by the wild-haired Marty Allen, are out to burgle the famous Gemini diamond from corrupt tycoon Victor Rosso (Lom). The circumlocutions of the plot are as boggling as the 600-foot-high cliffs [that] underpin the movie's final chase scene. It's great fun, though, and all set in the colorful island of Malta."

The Love War, March 10, 1970

Sci-fi, anyone? This pic, produced by Aaron Spelling and directed by George McCowan, who left his name on it (see *The Challenge*), offers another unique battle that presaged the *Alien vs. Predator* big-screen series: two alien races bent on taking over Earth (aren't they all?) conduct their battle here, with minimal forces, under our (human) noses; you can't see their alien skins unless you're wearing special glasses. Angie Dickinson stars as an unwitting earthling caught up in the war, and solid Lloyd Bridges is her savior. With Dan Travanty, later to become better known as Daniel J. Travanti on *Hill Street Blues*. The *Fairbanks* (Alaska) *Daily News-Miner* described the action thusly: "Kyle (Bridges) is a passenger aboard a bus heading north along the California coast. Sandy (Dickinson), a bitter young woman out of funds, flags down the bus on the highway. On reaching his destination, both realize they cannot simply walk away from each other. Kyle then tells Sandy that her life may be in danger. The tiny California town is to be the site of a battle in which the future of the world is at stake, and he is a combatant."

• Horror master John Carpenter used a similar "special way to see the aliens" gimmick in a later theatrical film: 1988's *They Live*, in which wrestler Roddy Piper discovers eyeglasses that show him our lives are a fascist nightmare controlled by an alien race.

The Young Country, March 17, 1970

A rascally gambler (Roger Davis) searches for the heir to a treasure in this amiable Western action flick with a game cast, including Walter Brennan, Joan Hackett, Peter Duel, and Wally Cox in a dual role as gunslinger Aaron Grimes (!) and "Ira Greebe." Cox got the best MOTW character names! Had this become a series, Davis and Duel would have co-starred, which is ironic, since Davis ended up replacing Duel on *Alias Smith and Jones*. See that entry for details.

Season Two: 1970–1971

How awful is Allan (Tony Perkins, at the top of the stairs)? Only sis Julie Harris knows … or does she?
Photofest

How Awful About Allan, September 22, 1970

Is Allan psychotic, or is someone actually trying to kill him, or frame him for his father's death a few years before this TV-movie starts? As played by the ever-twitching Tony Perkins, one is tempted to vote for *psycho*, pun intended, but watch this and spend a tingling 70-odd minutes with Perkins and a grand cast including the always watchable Julie Harris and the ever-present (in 1970s TV) Joan Hackett. Allan returns home years after an accidental fire (or was it?) killed his dad, burned his sister (Harris plays the part with a plastic mask covering part of her face), and left him institutionalized. Now psychosomatically blind, Allan is terrified by strange, whispering voices and the fear that someone is trying to kill him. Again, we're talking Allan here, *not* Perkins....

The Post-Register of Idaho Falls noted, "Hoping to assuage the guilt, Allan returns from the state hospital to live [with] Katherine (Harris) and Olive (Hackett). Katherine and Olive are convinced that Allan has lost his sanity as well as his eyesight." *The Charleston* (West Virginia) *Gazette* opined, "The second season of 90-minute movies made-for-TV opens with a run-of-the-mill horror story aimed at sending chills up your spine. ... We won't give away the plot, but mystery fans will have little trouble figuring out the eerie goings-on in the house with the burned-out bedroom and the dark shadows on the back stairway."

I say ... Perkins, Harris, and Hackett can keep me entertained any time. Another great slice of cheese brought to you by Aaron Spelling.

• Written by Henry Farrell (*Whatever Happened to Baby Jane?*) and directed by Curtis Harrington (*What's the Matter with Helen?*). Whatever happened to gothic horror films with classic Hollywood leading ladies slumming it and chewing the scenery?

Night Slaves, September 29, 1970

Though the title sounds like an exploitation flick, this MOTW is, in fact, a traditional "terror in a small town" tale, starring James Franciscus as a recovering car-accident victim (with a metal plate in his head) who, with wife Lee Grant, stumbles on some weird goings-on in a small town out west. Are the townspeople zombies? If not, then who—or what—is controlling their behavior? Franciscus' convenient metal plate prevents him from being affected. With Leslie Nielsen playing it straight as the sheriff; Ann Sothern's daughter Tisha Sterling as … well, we won't tell; Andrew Prine as the village idiot;1940s horror/thriller staple Elisha Cook Jr.; and Sharon "Christine Cagney" Gless in a small role that marked her TV debut. *The Lowell* (Massachusetts) *Sun* said, "*Night Slaves* on *Movie of the Week* is a good one, so it can be forgiven a few loose ends and a letdown at the end. It's mysterious and scary and handled in such a way that it's a long time before you know whether you are watching a science-fiction tale, or the mental breakdown of a man recovering from a car crash."

• Both *Cagney & Lacey* (Gless and Tyne Daly) cut their teeth in MOTWs before they hit it big in prime time. Daly's first MOTW was *In Search of America*, March 23, 1971.

But I Don't Want to Get Married, October 6, 1970

This chestnut about a recent widower (Herschel Bernardi) who finds himself the object of affection by many different single women is entertaining on a sitcom level, but distinguished mostly by its cast of well-known female faces, including Tina Louise, Joyce Van Patten, Shirley Jones, June Lockhart, Nanette Fabray, Kathleen Freeman, and Florence Halop. It also features one of the few post-*Lolita* appearances by former nymphet Sue Lyon. Hal Erikson of the online *All Movie Guide* notes the film "rolls along with TV-sitcom efficiency"

… which makes sense, since this MOTW was directed by *The Dick Van Dyke Show*'s neighbor, Jerry Paris (who played Jerry Helper on the show and also directed most of the series' episodes). Paris followed his acting career with a prolific stint directing sitcoms, TV movies, and big-screen films. His sitcom directing credits include *Here's Lucy*, *The Mary Tyler Moore Show*, *The Odd Couple*, and *The New Dick Van Dyke Show*. He also directed seven other MOTWs, including *Call Her Mom* and *The Feminist and the Fuzz*. Paris died in 1986.

The Old Man Who Cried Wolf, October 13, 1970
Classic Hollywood gangster Edward G. Robinson, in his final TV appearance (and one of his final film appearances) plays a senior citizen (or "old man," as the character was described back then) who is beaten unconscious while visiting old friend Sam Jaffe. When Robinson awakens, Jaffe is dead (by "natural causes," Robinson is told) and no one believes his story of an attack. What could have been a routine suspense tale is elevated to extremely enjoyable, thanks to Robinson's deft performance.

*Wild Women, October 20, 1970
What do you do when a job is dangerous—possibly a suicide mission? Enlist five female convicts to act as your cover story. In this case "it" is smuggling arms into Mexican-occupied Texas, circa 1840, just when the United States was getting ready to annex the land. Stalwart Hugh O'Brien is aided by, among others, luscious Anne Francis; B-movie and character actress Marie Windsor; Marilyn Maxwell; and Danny Thomas' former TV daughter, Sherry Jackson. The five female convicts are in it to win their freedom by posing as the wives of army engineers and would-be settlers, but actually trying to get troops over the Mexican border.

• Francis had already gained wild-woman cred as the knockout detective heroine (she was gorgeous *and* could kick ass, *and* had a pet ocelot) of the cult series *Honey West* (1965), for which she a Golden Globe in 1965 (and was nominated for an Emmy). Dick Kleiner in *The Daily Times-News* of Burlington, N.C., on August 4, 1970 noted "Anne's been busy. First, she adopted a baby girl, Margaret West Francis. West is an old family name and has nothing to do with *Honey West*, Anne's old series.... There's talk of [*Wild Women*] becoming a series. Anne's heard the talk but, 'I don't really think I want another series now,' she says. 'You just can't be a parent and a series star at the same time.'" Francis needn't have worried. *Wild Women* never made it to series. At press time in 2008, 77-year-old Francis (best remembered for *West* and her two fifties film classics, *Forbidden Planet* and *Bad Day at Black Rock*) was battling lung cancer.

The House That Would Not Die, October 27, 1970

This was a nice addition to the haunted house genre. Ruth Bennett (Barbara Stanwyck) goes to live with her niece Sara (Kitty Winn of *The Exorcist*) in an old Amish house inherited from a relative. Guess what? There's something horribly wrong with the house, and it has to do with a couple of Revolutionary War-era spirits, an old diary, and ... murder. A ghost called Ammie (for Amanda) possesses Sara during a séance. Ammie wants to right a very old wrong. The best thing about the movie is that it relies on the writing and actors, not gore or special effects, to thrill the viewer, and succeeds more often than not. Mabel Albertson (Darrin's befuddled mom on *Bewitched*) plays Babs' neighbor.

The North Adams (Massachusetts) *Transcript* chose *House* as a Best Bet the night it aired, and wrote, "If you like chilling tales of haunted houses and mysterious doings, *The House*

That Wouldn't Die … is must viewing. It's a beauty of an old-fashioned thriller with Barbara Stanwyck and Katherine [Kitty] Winn as aunt and niece, who come to an old house which Miss Stanwyck has inherited. Her neighbor is Richard Egan, an anthropology professor. Michael Anderson Jr. is his young friend. These four are intimately involved [with an] evil presence in the house, a presence which possesses both Egan and Miss Winn. There are some marvelous effects here, when the house seems to come alive with unseen dangers, and the sound effects man had a great time [creating] the whistling of the wind. Miss Winn, who is excellent in her role, is a member of ACT (American Conservatory Theater), a San Francisco repertory company. Doreen Lang, as a medium, and Mabel Albertson as Egan's aunt, complete the cast."

•Based on the book *Ammie, Come Home*, by Barbara Michaels, originally published in 1969. The title phrase was hauntingly called throughout the film by the ghost of Ammie's father, a general suspected of treason, as he roamed the house and grounds, seeking his long-lost daughter.

Tribes, November 10, 1970

Poster Tagline: Wanted by the U.S. Marines … For AWOL … Insubordination … and doing his own thing [!]

Another well-remembered MOTW, *Tribes* featured Jan-Michael Vincent at his hottest, as Adrian, a surly hippie Marine drafted to serve in Vietnam. The movie follows his training, and, naturally, he can't abide by the rules. Pretty much a PG-rated homoerotic sadist-masochist study, Adrian gets into trouble time and again, and keeps getting punished by sergeants Earl Holliman and especially drill instructor Darren McGavin. But his spirit cannot be broken and his survival methods are eventually adopted by his fellow recruits. *Tribes* gets points for its acting and its (for the time) risqué plot:

hippies vs. the establishment, a rare vote for peace in a year of violent Vietnam protests and the Kent State shootings.

War stories were popular MOTW subjects. Here, DI Darren McGavin ain't taking no you-know-what from drafted hippie Jan-Michael Vincent in *Tribes*. Photofest

• Vincent often played the youthful admirer/apprentice to older macho stars like Charles Bronson (*The Mechanic*) and Burt Reynolds (*Hooper*). And just prior to *Tribes*, he played a sexy, often half-naked adventurer marooned on an island with several others and fighting pirates on the campy serial *Danger Island*, a segment of the surreal *The Banana Splits Adventure Hour*. He was billed as Michael Vincent.

• Writer Tracy Keenan Wynn won an Emmy for *Tribes* and another in 1974 for adapting *The Autobiography of Miss Jane Pittman*. He is the son of actor Keenan Wynn, and the grandson of comic Ed Wynn.

• Parts of the movie were filmed at San Diego's Marine Corps Recruit Depot.

Crowhaven Farm, November 24, 1970

A young couple (Hope Lange and Paul Burke) inherits a home in Salem, Massachusetts (Witch Alert!) and moves in with the hope of saving their marriage, but the union is further put to the test when (Duh!) strange things begin happening on the farm. It all has to do with a witchy ancestor of Lange's, who wasn't so nice to the rest of her coven some 200 years before. Are the descendents of those witches trying to wreak revenge, or is Lange just going mad? And she seemed so nice! *The Lowell* (Massachusetts) *Sun*, noted in its TV listings that, "Evil is afoot on *Crowhaven Farm*. It's a scary tale about witches, which is ultimately too close to *Rosemary's Baby* for comfort. Hope Lange is the innocent, a wife who will do 'anything' to have a child with Paul Burke, her artist husband. She inherits a Massachusetts farm, a colorful place where she has frightening visions and even worse dreams. Investigation proves that events of the past are happening again. Lloyd Bochner plays a neighbor with an eye for Miss Lange, Cindy Eilbacher (regularly Hal Holbrook's daughter on *The Bold Ones*) is a child too sweet to he real." Yet another movie that proved early on the MOTW knew how to make genuine chillers.

• Lange was haunted by a friendlier ghost (handsome Edward Mulhare as Capt. Daniel Clegg) in her sitcom, *The Ghost and Mrs. Muir*, and won two Emmys for it. She was nominated for a third Emmy as best dramatic actress in 1973 for the MOTW *That Certain Summer* (see Season Five).

Run Simon, Run, December 1, 1970

Just prior to becoming a big-screen superstar, Burt Reynolds played a Native American just out of prison, having served 10 years for his brother's murder. He, of course, is not the real killer, so he's out to avenge his brother's death. When he returns to his Papago Indian reservation, he discovers changes, and not for the better: tribal custom has been abandoned for commercialism, and his tribesmen are not inclined to do anything about it. Plus, they get drunk a lot. He becomes chief and wants to give pride back to his nation, but a conflict arises when he falls for pretty Inger Stevens (who had dated Reynolds), in her final film appearance. Stevens played a rich socially responsible white person who happened to be the government Indian agent. Reynolds gave a brooding, intense performance using few lines of dialogue. The movie was filmed in Tucson, Arizona and was an Aaron Spelling production.

• Stevens was adept at comedy and drama; in her short career she was best known as the title character of the sitcom *The Farmer's Daughter* (1963–'66). She was reportedly depressed about her relationship with Reynolds when she was found dead, a probable suicide, in April 1970, eight months before the airing of this movie.

• Reynolds was already starring in the series *Dan August* (1971–'72), and got his big-screen break in *Deliverance* (1972) soon after.

Weekend of Terror, December 8, 1970

What, I ask you, could be more devastating and compelling than nuns in trouble?! Especially when the nuns in question are the comely Carol Lynley, Lois Nettleton, and the lovable Jane Wyatt (the three-time Emmy-winning mom of *Father Knows Best*)? Not much. Throw in Robert Conrad and Lee Majors at the height of their appeal, as ex-cons and would be kidnappers, and you've got a campy, melodramatic winner. When the guys' original hostage is accidentally killed, Sister Ellen (Nettleton) is forced to shed her habit and replace the victim she resembles, while her fellow sisters in faith, Lynley and Wyatt—also held captive—question their religious devotion.

The Man Who Wanted to Live Forever, December 15, 1970

Though this medical drama had a plot right out of a 1950s B-movie—wealthy old man (Burl Ives) uses research foundation to try to extend his life—this one was handled nicely and benefits from performances by two Oscar winners: Ives and Sandy Dennis (in a rare non-eccentric and effective performance as, don't laugh, a hematologist). Stuart Whitman is Dennis' love interest, a brilliant heart surgeon (aren't they all?) at a private research center (isolated, of course—the better for Ives to fund his life-altering experiments without interruptions). The pair discovers that, rather than doing good for mankind, as they thought, Ives is using them and others at the center as guinea pigs for his research.

* **Alias Smith and Jones**, January 5, 1971

Gorgeous duo Peter Duel and Ben Murphy played Butch and Sundance-types shanghaied into working for the law. A potentially successful series—which debuted 16 days after this pilot, on January 21, 1971—was cut short by Duel's suicide in December 1971. The role was recast with handsome Roger Davis (a friend of Duel's who took over almost immediately; see below) but the Duel-Murphy chemistry was gone, and the show only lasted another 17 episodes. Co-starring Sally Field; Duel had a recurring role on her earlier series, *Gidget* (1965–'66).

Ben Murphy and Peter Duel are having a high old time in the Wild West in *Alias Smith and Jones*. This pilot went straight to series, but Duel's suicide cut short the series' run. Photofest

• The troubled Duel once referred to a role on a weekly series as "…a big fat drag … it's the ultimate trap."
• In order to salvage exterior footage shot without dialogue that Duel had filmed before his death, vocal actor and impersonator Paul Frees (*Rocky & Bullwinkle*, *The Flintstones*, *George of the Jungle*, and hundreds of other voice jobs) was called in to loop the late actor's voice in post-production.
• UPI's Vernon Scott wrote, in a January 25, 1972, syndicated article, about Davis being "troubled by public reaction to his

presence in the series, for several reasons. 'Somebody had to take the part,' said the Kentucky-born Davis. 'I probably have some guilt feelings attached to something good happening to me as the result of a friend's death. Anybody would feel that way. I just wish it weren't necessary.'"

Scott noted that, "Duel killed himself New Year's Eve. January 1, Universal Studios located Davis at Aspen, Colorado, and asked him to return to Hollywood Friday and stand by. By Saturday, ABC and Universal decided he was their man. Sunday, Davis was in wardrobe. Monday he was before the cameras. Ironically, Davis and Duel were close friends. 'I had seen Pete in the show the night he killed himself,' Roger said, a note of sadness in his voice. 'I'd been over to his house three weeks earlier. We'd gotten to know one another very well when we did a television movie that was supposed to be a pilot for a new series [almost] two years ago. It was *The Young Country* [see separate entry in Season One]. We've been friends ever since.'

"Davis had previously played lead roles on the tube, Scott reported, "and was, in fact, a guest star last year on *Alias Smith and Jones*, playing a heavy…. He is a warm, dignified man who gives the impression of being a straight shooter. Clearly he has courage. His decision to step in for Peter Duel was not an easy one. He will be judged Feb. 3 when his first episode in the show is aired." Duel's final episode had aired January 27.

• Universal Studios' TV division, having decided not to partner with ABC when the MOTW series debuted, finally jumped on the bandwagon—nothing like strong ratings to change a studio's mind—with this movie, and many others to come.

Assault on the Wayne, January 12, 1971
Nuclear submarine drama finds the vessel's captain, played by Leonard Nimoy, becoming ill (and slowly going mad?) in

the midst of sabotage. Joseph Cotten, Keenan Wynn, Sam Elliott, William Windom, and Lloyd Haynes (*Room 222*) co-star. *The Panama City* (Florida) *News-Herald* called this "a gripping adventure story of international intrigue" featuring "a deadly battle of wits [and] suspenseful drama" aboard the sub, while the *Albuquerque* (New Mexico) *Journal* reported the film had "an excellent, detailed set and a competent cast of reliable actors who give this standard espionage yarn aboard a nuclear sub a lift…. Nimoy is all stiffness-and-orders as the commander of the sub who discovers that some members of his crew are working for a foreign power. The climax plays like a Hardy Boys' adventure, but action fans won't complain." Maybe the Hardy Boys should…

• Nimoy and Windom had faced off before in a famous episode of the original *Star Trek*, "The Doomsday Machine."

Dr. Cook's Garden, January 19, 1971

Horror was a major theme of many of the MOTWs and this one was a doozy. Young doctor (Frank Converse) returns to his Vermont hometown to practice, and discovers his mentor (Bing Crosby, of all people) is taking the life-and-death matters of his patients into his own hands. "Bad" people die early, and "good" people live longer. Converse's request to take over the ailing Dr. Cook's practice is declined, and when the younger doc does some investigating, he finds out a bit too much for Dr. Cook's liking, such as what the mysterious letter "R" means on certain deceased patient charts. Converse is, not surprisingly, soon in danger himself. This film is most notable for featuring Blythe Danner as Dr. Cook's nurse and Converse's love interest in one of her early roles. In its anticipation of right-to-die issues, this movie was ahead of its time.

• Based on a play by Ira (*Rosemary's Baby*) Levin that starred Burl Ives (why wasn't *he* cast in this MOTW?) and Keir Dullea, which closed after eight Broadway performances in September 1967, but became a stock/regional theater staple.

• **Spoilers!** The "R" stands for Removed, which is what Dr. Cook's been doing to those patients he deems unworthy of living. And can you guess what's fertilizing the doc's meticulous garden?

The Feminist and the Fuzz, January 26, 1971

The MOTW roster included more than its share of flicks with themes reflecting what was going on in society at the time, but this being network TV in 1971, the issues (in this case, the feminist movement) were mostly handled with kid gloves. In fact, the New York *Daily News* reviewed this flick as a setback for women's lib. Doctor Barbara Eden has to room with male chauvinist cop David Hartman (before he switched from actor to anchorman); wacky fun ensues, and everyone learns to get along a little better. Most of the fun is provided by its vintage-1970s cast, including Jo Anne Worley, Julie Newmar, John McGiver, Herb Edelman, and Harry Morgan, plus Farrah Fawcett. Penny Marshall and Sheila James had small roles as "Liberation Ladies." *The Edwardsville* (Illinois) *Intelligencer* reported, "If you're tired of TV's relevance and you just want to relax and be entertained, try *The Feminist and the Fuzz* tonight. Filmed on location in San Francisco, it's a wacky comedy that is beautifully cast. Barbara Eden is a lady doctor and feminist. Desperate to obtain an apartment, she winds up making a deal with David Hartman, a gentleman she calls a 'cop-lawyer-sexual-bigot-Boy Scout,' to share an apartment. From this all kinds of complications build to a very funny climactic scene which also involves Harry Morgan, as Barbara's bewildered father, Julie Newmar, very funny as a prostitute about to become 'an X-rated movie star,' and 1995 *Playboy* centerfold Farrah Fawcett as Hartman's girl. There's also a wild scene that was filmed in the Playboy Club, in which pretty Barbara wears the teeniest of bikinis. Others in the cast: Jo Anne Worley and her real life escort, Roger Perry, who here plays a doctor who makes all kinds of cracks about Miss Worley." Who could resist the latter?

• Perry and Worley got tired of just "escorting" each other around and were married in 1975; they divorced 25 years later.

• James, of *Dobie Gillis* fame, subsequently revealed she was gay, and got a law degree specializing in—you guessed it—feminist causes. She was elected a California state assemblyperson and Senator.

The Point, February 2, 1971

A true original, *The Point* was written by Harry Nilsson, who also provided the words and music to this animated tale—a story that a father tells his son—of a round-headed boy (Oblio) and his dog (Arrow) who lived in a town called Point where everything, except Oblio, came to a point—including the people. Oblio's head was round, and he was banished to the Pointless forest, where he learns that you don't have to literally have a pointed head to make a point. Bobby Brady himself, Mike Lookinland, voiced Oblio, and the narrator of the MOTW (and the father in the story) was Dustin Hoffman. Paul Frees—the legendary voice talent who dubbed Pete Duel after his suicide in the MOTW *Alias Smith and Jones*—voiced Oblio's father and others in the story-within-a-story.

• Apparently Hoffman agreed only to a one-time participation. Ringo Starr was dubbed as the narrator of the home video version (Alan Barzman narrated the second telecast, and Alan Thicke narrated a third telecast on the Disney Channel).

Whoever narrated, the story remained a charming fairy tale with a real, er, point.

• Nilsson's biggest pop hit was "Everybody's Talking" from the movie *Midnight Cowboy*. He also wrote and sang the infectious theme to the TV series *The Courtship of Eddie's Father* and had a novelty hit with the ditty "Coconut."

• If you've been to Disney World or Disneyland, you may have heard Frees as the voice of the "Ghost Host" leading you into the popular Haunted Mansion attraction.

Love, Hate, Love, February 9, 1971

A routine romance between a fashion model (Lesley Ann Warren) and a playboy engineer (Ryan O'Neal) turns ugly when her psychotic fiancé (Peter Haskell) won't let go. This early, chilling treatment of stalking was quite well done, and without the excess violence or gore that has come to typify this kind of tale. *The Berkshire Eagle* (Pittsfield, Mass.) called the film a "good gripper," and wrote of a repeat showing in 1973, "A good performance by Haskell as a relentless rich man with sadistic tendencies is the main attraction of this made-for-TV feature suspense film. Haskell loses pretty Lesley Warren to handsome Ryan O'Neal and then makes their lives miserable by dogging their every move, even cross-country to California. The suspense builds nicely and Haskell's menacing presence will send chills up most viewer's backs."

Maybe I'll Come Home in the Spring, February 16, 1971

Generation-gap fever! (Well, it was 1971, what did you expect?) Earnest Sally Field, who left her alcoholic parents (Jackie Cooper and Eleanor Parker) and drug-addicted sister (Lane Bradbury) in the suburbs to experience the hippie life, returns (for somewhat muddled reasons) to find they haven't changed a bit. Now little sis wants to leave. Lots of screaming and angst shove this one over the top. Watch for David Carradine as Flack, a hippie leader Field befriended on her journey.

• Parker and Field played sisters (!) a short year-and-a-half later, albeit oldest and youngest siblings, in one of my favorite MOTWs, *Home for the Holidays* (see Season Four).

• Reviewing the movie the next day in the *Cedar Rapids* (Iowa) *Gazette*, Television Today columnist Rick DuBrow called it, "an ambitious teleplay about a runaway girl who returns to her suburban, respectable home after a fling at hippie life" and that Field gave "a sensitive performance as the girl—a youngster, not overly intellectual, who is trying to set her life in order after failing to find peace of mind with either her family or the hippie existence.

"Unfortunately, she has not come home to paradise. Her younger sister envies her hippie experience and is anxious to emulate her—partly for the same reason that drove Miss Field away: The lack of understanding or communication from her parents. In addition, the father and mother, portrayed by Jackie Cooper and Eleanor Parker, run a very tense household and seem to have learned little or nothing from their experience with their runaway daughter."

DuBrow found fault with just one aspect of the drama: "[Field]'s role was most effective because it showed the subtle and not-so-subtle pulls of both sides in her mind and avoided being oversimplified. The envious sister also was fleshed out convincingly by Lane Bradbury. Yet the parents, once again, were those stereotyped, black-and-white suburban villains we see repeatedly in video drama." As he points out, "when you go for 'types' rather than multidimensional characters, you sacrifice the opportunity to delve into the subtleties that make drama less predictable and thus more revealing and compassionate."

Personally, I much prefer an emotionally wrought Eleanor Parker in any given situation, stereotyped character or not.

Longstreet, February 23,1971

By 1971, the detective genre had already been done to death on TV, so, looking for a new angle, James Franciscus was cast as a *blind* detective. He was formerly an insurance investigator, until someone blew him up along with his wife, who did not survive. What else could he do, but turn sleuth and find those responsible? Franciscus was handsome and talented enough to keep us interested for 23 one-hour episodes after this pilot movie. The series didn't make it past the 1971–'72 season.

• But … veteran writer/producer Steven Bochco (*Hill Street Blues*, *Cop Rock*) liked the basic concept: In 2005, Ron Eldard starred in *Blind Justice*, a police drama in which his character, Detective Dunbar, who was blinded in the line of duty, returns to the force with a Seeing Eye dog.

Yuma, March 2, 1971

Filmed in Tucson, Arizona, this old-fashioned Western is a sturdy, if somewhat predictable, vehicle for sturdy Clint Walker as a marshal sent to clean up the town of Yuma. He would have cleaned up every week, along with co-star Kathryn Hays, except the pilot wasn't picked up. Featuring Barry Sullivan, Edgar Buchanan (*Petticoat Junction*), Morgan Woodward, and Peter Mark Richman. *The Florence* (South Carolina) *Morning News* called *Yuma* "a hard-hitting western adventure … set in Arizona territory in the 1870s. Dave Harmon (Walker) is the frontier town's new U.S. Marshal. While trying to stop a barroom brawl, he is forced to kill a cattleman, Sam King (Bruce Glover), and jail his brother, Rol (Neil Russell). That night, someone lets Rol out of jail and as he flees he is killed by a bullet from Harmon's rifle. The surviving King brother,

Arch (Woodward), vows vengeance on the marshal unless he can prove he did not shoot Rol. As Harmon tries to unravel the plot to discredit him, he comes to suspect Nels Decker (Sullivan), operator of a local freight line."

• Walker had starred for many years on the Western series *Cheyenne* (1955-'63), the first hour-long Western on TV—and this was his return to the genre after an eight-year absence that included several appearances as Lucy Carmichael's (Lucille Ball) boyfriend on *The Lucy Show*. Walker also appeared in the MOTWs *Killdozer* and *Scream of the Wolf*, both in early 1974 (see Season Five).

• Hays is well remembered for her turn as Gem, an "empath," on the original *Star Trek*, and a long-running stint on the soap opera *As the World Turns*.

*__*River of Gold*__, March 9, 1971

Ray Milland hams it up as an evil millionaire (is there any other kind in these MOTWs?) after sunken treasure off the coast of Acapulco. Suzanne Pleshette (How do we love her? Let us count the ways) teams up with hunky divers Dack Rambo and Roger Davis to find same. Once more into the sea, dear friends, once more (see *Black Water Gold*, Season One). The series, had it become one, would have followed Rambo and Davis as they dove around the world, romancing and finding adventure.

• Davis cemented his hunk status in 1964 alongside fellow beefcakes Fabian and Tab Hunter, and beach babes Shelley Fabares and Barbara Eden, in the surf, sand, and implied teen sex epic *Ride the Wild Surf*.

• Rambo was one-half of a gorgeous set of identical twins. The other, Dirk (their real first names were much worse: Norman and Orman, respectively), also an actor, was killed by a drunk driver in 1967 at the age of 25. Dack continued acting through the 1990s, and died of AIDS in 1994.

In Search of America, March 23, 1971
Shades of *The Partridge Family*: A groovy lad with hippie sensibilities (Jeff Bridges in an early role) convinces his more conventional family (Carl Betz and Vera Miles are the parents) to look for the real America by traveling cross-country on an old bus with him. Come to think of it, the Partridge bus was way cooler. Critic John J. O'Connor, in *The New York Times*, called *In Search of America* "ludicrous" and "painfully well-meaning," but added "Trite? You'd better believe it. Insignificant? Hardly. When the dropout message of the counter-culture becomes a vehicle of mass entertainment in prime television time, a long road has been traveled in an incredibly short time. The journey might be questioned but it can't be dismissed." The journey was short, as this pilot never sold. A fabulous supporting cast included Howard Duff, Kim Hunter, Sal Mineo, Tyne Daly, and Glynn Turman.

• Betz is best remembered as the all-American dad on *The Donna Reed Show*, which ran from 1958–'66. His character, Dr. Alex Stone, was voted number 16 in a June 2004 *TV Guide* list of the "50 Greatest TV Dads of all Time." He subsequently won Emmy and Golden Globe awards for his starring role in the law series *Judd for the Defense* (1967–'69). He died in 1978 at the age of 56.

*The Sheriff, March 30, 1971

Venturing once again into "ripped from the headlines" territory, and ripping off more than a little of the plot from the classic *To Kill a Mockingbird*, this MOTW took on the same two hot-button issues: prejudice and rape. A small-town black sheriff (Ossie Davis) and his white deputy (Kaz Garas) look into the case of a white businessman (Ross Martin of *The Wild, Wild West*) accused of raping a black co-ed. The cast features Davis' real-life wife, Ruby Dee, as his reel wife, plus Kyle Johnson (son of *Star Trek*'s Nichelle Nichols) as their son; Lynda Day George as Garas' prejudiced Southern wife; Brenda Sykes as the alleged victim; and Moses Gunn as her father. The series would have focused on the sheriff (Davis), his deputy (Garas), and their families. *The Edwardsville* (Illinois) *Intelligencer* reported, "*The Sheriff*, set in mythical Loma [and filmed in Santa Paula, California] ... builds to a crisp courtroom scene which is fairly explicit in some of its dialogue. The major question to be answered: Was it rape or did the girl, as Martin says, consent: There are some bits of social significance here but mainly it's a well-paced adventure yarn."

• The blaxploitation flick *...tick... tick... tick...* (1970) also featured a black sheriff (Jim Brown) in unfriendly territory (the South).

*Escape, April 6, 1971

For its second-season finale, the MOTW ran a pilot with ties to many different genres: sci-fi, horror, drama, action, and detective, to name a few. Christopher George is a P.I. and escape artist after a madman who has a virus that will turn people into zombies. Uh, oh. (Well, have you ever met a *good* zombie?) A press release made it sound more exciting: "A master escape artist battles a criminal mastermind who has abducted a scientist with knowledge that could doom the entire human race." The series would have had George and comic relief Avery Schreiber helping someone in trouble every week, but apparently not enough of us wanted to see that. With TV perennial William Schallert (Patty Duke's dad on her sitcom), Oscar winner Gloria Grahame, and Bowery Boy Huntz Hall.

• William Windom, who plays the "mad doctor" here, was better known at the time as the courtly congressman on *The Farmer's Daughter*. He'd recently (1970) won an Emmy for the innovative sitcom *My World and Welcome to It*—which blended live action and animated sequences—based on the life of humorist and cartoonist James Thurber. Windom went on to become a longtime semiregular on the series *Murder, She Wrote* (1985-'96). He starred or co-starred in many other MOTWs, including *A Taste of Evil* (1971), *Second Chance* (1972), *A Great American Tra*gedy (1972), and *The Abduction of St. Anne* (1975).

Season Three: 1971-1972

The Forgotten Man, September 14, 1971

Dennis Weaver plays a soldier presumed dead in Vietnam who turns up years later to discover—surprise!—everything about his old life has changed. Interesting as an artifact of the times and for the excellent cast, including Anne Francis, Lois Nettleton, plus the essential child star of the era, Pamelyn Ferdin (See *Daughter of the Mind* in Season One for more on Ferdin). Season One's *The Ballad of Andy Crocker* had a similar theme.

• In an interview in the *Bridgeport* (Connecticut) *Sunday Post* a month after this movie aired (October 17), headlined "Dennis Weaver Hopes McCloud Will Get Chester Off His Back," the actor bemoaned being typecast for so many years on *Gunsmoke* as the gimpy Chester, famous for his drawling "Mis-ter Dill-on" when he addressed his boss. (He won a supporting actor Emmy for the role in 1958.) With a full season of his detective series *McCloud* under his belt and heading into season two, Weaver, then a Screen Actor's Guild board member, believed "all those old jokes about his limp are finally receding into the background … 'They are beginning to think of me now as McCloud,'" he told the paper. Roles such as the Vietnam vet in this MOTW—and his upcoming portrayal of the harried driver in the classic *Duel* (see November 13)—also helped the public accept Weaver as much more than Marshal Dillon's assistant. Weaver later served as SAG president (1973-'75).

The Birdmen, September 18, 1971

Tagline: They used to boast there were only two ways to escape from Hitler's Beckstadt prison: to die … or to sprout wings.

Within days of each other, the first two films of the MOTW's third season were mired in war stories, first Vietnam, and then World War II with this escape drama, featuring Doug McClure, Richard Basehart, Rene Auberjonois, Chuck Connors, Tom Skerritt, and, in a rare departure from his signature role of Jethro in *The Beverly Hillbillies*, Max Baer Jr. McClure is an American sent to Europe to rescue a scientist working on the A-bomb, but both get caught and imprisoned on the Germany/Swiss border. How to escape? By making a hang glider for two, of course—in prison, out of fabric and bed frame, then hiding it until the escape. Also known as *Escape of the Birdmen*.

• Based loosely on the book *Escape from Colditz*, by P.R. Reid, which was in turn based on real-life incidents (in reality the glider was built, but the prison was liberated before it could be used).

Congratulations, It's a Boy!, September 21, 1971

From war overseas, the MOTW shifted focus to war on the home front … domestic war, that is. Bill Bixby stepped out of his concurrent, popular role of widowed father with young son on *The Courtship of Eddie's Father* (1969-'72) to play a swinging, carefree bachelor who suddenly discovers he's got a teenage son. Bixby accepts parental responsibility, but tries to keep his son hidden; after all, the phrase *carefree bachelor* doesn't exactly equate with *single father*. Hilarity ensues. The best stuff here comes courtesy of old pros Ann Sothern and Jack Albertson as Bixby's folks. Also known as *So's Your Old Man!*

• Diane Baker, Bixby's co-star, told Leona Pappas of *The San Antonio Express* that, "Bill is usually thought of as a comedian.

He has sensitivity and great feeling. It was an experience working with him on this story ... very interesting and entertaining." Baker also expressed the desire to have her own TV series, as "I became aware more and more that television is a medium many more people are watching." Though she guest-starred on TV more than 80 times in her career, she never got that long-running series.

Five Desperate Women, September 28, 1971

Five women—Anjanette Comer, Joan Hackett, Denise Nicholas, Stefanie Powers and Julie Sommars, college buddies who've been planning a reunion for five years—finally go on their vacation together. Just the five of them, on a secluded island. Things have changed since college, and they find themselves not getting along, and realizing that their lives might not have become what they expected them to. But their petty arguments become a moot point when one of them is murdered. They are the only ones there—except for the possibly insane handyman (Bradford Dillman in the type of menacing role he could do in his sleep), and the muscular but mysterious captain of their boat, Robert Conrad (who might be missing some marbles himself). Whodunnit? I'll never tell, but this atmospheric, taut suspenser had a profound effect on me; it was the first time I remember watching someone get murdered by drowning on-screen, and it seemed so real it creeped me out for months. Lights on for this one.

Sweet, Sweet Rachel, October 2, 1971

One of the genres the MOTW excelled at was suspense, and this flick is a typically strong entry in that category. Rachel (Stefanie Powers) is, according to ABC's press release, "the wife of a wealthy music promoter. After a night out alone, Rachel returns to her coastal mansion in time to see her husband hurl himself out of a window to the rocks below. To her horror, it was an eerie apparition of herself that beckoned her husband to his death." Her physician does what any sensible doc would do in the same sitch: recommends her to an expert on ESP and the supernatural, played by Alex Dreier. The latter recreates the events leading up the husband's death and almost dies in the same manner. Is someone with fantastic extra-sensory powers trying to drive Rachel mad? The always reliable Louise Latham, Pat Hingle and John Hillerman are on hand to spice up the proceedings.

The Last Child, October 5, 1971

The future of 1994 is grim. Michael Cole (*Mod Squad*) and wife Janet Margolin find this out firsthand because they want to have a second child. The first one died, but that makes no difference in this bleak vision of life in these United States, where overpopulation is the overriding concern (triggering a "no medical care" rule for those over 65). Van Heflin is one such senior who tries to help the youngsters cross the border to Canada and flee the Population Control Police (well, it was good enough for kids trying to escape being drafted into the Vietnam War). A picture of an America gone fascist, the story doesn't seem quite so futuristic anymore. This was Heflin's final film appearance; he had died a few months before it aired.

Thief, October 9, 1971

The always-wonderful Richard Crenna and Angie Dickinson star in this oft-used Hollywood tale of an in-debt thief forced to pull one last job before he can retire. *The Kennebec Journal* (Augusta, Maine) called the movie, "A good, simple, absorbing look at a *Thief*. Crenna plays the title role, a clever burglar who lives in a pleasant home, has a sexy woman (Dickinson) and a goal involving the custody of his son. He also has a good friend, a lawyer (Cameron Mitchell), who wants to help. But the thief is basically a weak man who can't quite stick to the goal. This was filmed completely on location (producer Ron Roth says he thinks actual locales always help actors and indeed the performances are fine here), in the San Fernando Valley, Beverly Hills and Reno. Hurd Hatfield, as the thief's elegant fence and Robert Webber as a man to whom the thief owes a large sum of money, are also in the good cast. There are several ironies scattered throughout the script, leading to a final one which gives the show a perfect ending. Ron Grainer gets a nod for an excellent score and John D. F. Black's screenplay is honest and realistic."

• The "former-thief-comes-out-of-retirement-to-pull-one-last-job" plot has been recycled often in Hollywood, with varied success, including *The Opportunists* (2000), *The Good Thief* (2002), and *After the Sunset* (2004).

A Taste of Evil, October 12, 1971

John Llewellyn Moxey, who directed a number of the horror- and terror-oriented MOTWs, scores here with a brooding tale about a young woman (Barbara Parkins) released from an asylum, who, under the care of her scary mother (Barbara Stanwyck, chewing the scenery) begins to see … dead people. Though not in the same league as *The Sixth Sense*, there is a twist at the end. William Windom and Roddy McDowall contribute to the fun. Still not convinced? *The Charleston* (West Virginia) *Gazette* noted, "If an old-fashioned mystery melodrama set in a big, rambling mansion where all the residents act like refugees from Madame Tussaud's [wax] horror museum appeals to you, then tune in. Lovely Barbara Parkins, the heroine of the piece, returns home … cured after years in a sanitarium following a childhood incident which left her catatonic, only to find herself terrorized almost from the word go. Barbara Stanwyck, looking every inch the regal matriarch she plays, gets a chance to rant and rave in the super-charged finale. Tune in for the two Barbaras doing their thing." I did, and I'd do it all over again.

In Broad Daylight, October 16, 1971

When Anthony Chappel (Richard Boone), former movie star and matinee idol blinded in an accident, discovers that his wife Elizabeth (Stella Stevens) is sleeping with his best friend, he decides to kill them both. Part of the complicated plan involves convincing those around him that he can see and disguising himself as a 70-year-old (that's where the "great actor" part comes in). The cast includes the ever-dependable Suzanne Pleshette as his therapist, John Marley and Whit Bissell. Stevens, at the time, was everyone's favorite player of sleazy women, or girls-gone-bad. The rugged Boone was best known as gun-for-hire Paladin in the TV Western *Have Gun, Will Travel*.

Suddenly Single, October 19, 1971

The plot is simple and threadbare: a divorced man has to readjust to being single. What elevates this one is a remarkable cast: Hal Holbrook, Barbara Rush, Agnes Moorehead, a surprisingly restrained Harvey Korman, Margot Kidder, Cloris Leachman, and Michael Constantine. *The Winnipeg Free Press* (Manitoba, Canada), raved: "A quality breakthrough in movies made for television will be readily apparent this week and Hal Holbrook carries the ball on two spectacular occasions. First he stars with Cloris Leachman and Barbara Rush in *Suddenly Single*, playing a divorced 38-year-old druggist." Holbrook commented that he played "the kind of role Jack Lemmon used to do." The other movie Holbrook was in that week was also a drama, *Goodbye, Raggedy Ann*, and the *Free Press* was so impressed with Holbrook's range it posited, "perhaps movie makers will tune in for an audition, and realize what they've been overlooking."

• Since Lemmon was very much alive and working steadily at the time, one can assume Holbrook was referring to the frothy, somewhat saucy comedies Lemmon made in the early 1960s. Lemmon himself had graduated to hard drama, and would win his second Oscar two years later (1973) for a very poignant performance in *Save the Tiger*.

Death Takes a Holiday, October 23, 1971

Monte Markham, as Death personified, provides the heat (as in hunk) and temptation to starlet Yvette Mimieux in this solid version of the classic film in which Death takes on human form to find out why people love life so much. (Simple answer: Maybe it's all we got?) Melvyn Douglas and Myrna Loy provide some old-Hollywood magic, and the (debatably) equally hot Bert Convy adds testosterone to the proceedings. President Reagan's daughter with Jane Wyman, Maureen, also makes an appearance. This MOTW is much better than the turgid, overlong remake, *Meet Joe Black* (1998), starring a pretty but peculiarly placid Brad Pitt.

• In an interview in the Lumberton, N.C., *Robesonian*, on September 26, 1976, coinciding with a repeat of this movie, Melvyn Douglas commented on the filming: "I remember being impressed with the play and then the [1934] movie with Fredric March. Death was played in a somewhat sinister fashion and his character was nebulous. He wore a cloak and there was a dark shadow around his head."

Douglas, the paper noted, "for over 40 years a noted stage and film actor ... never thinks of things in terms of best portrayals." The actor, who won an Emmy for *Do Not*

Go Gentle Into That Good Night and a supporting actor Oscar for the film *Hud*, told the paper, "I may enjoy doing one film more than another, but that's a different matter." As for the newer version of *Death Takes a Holiday*, Douglas said, "Our version is quite different. It's so updated, you'll hardly recognize it. Monte Markham, who plays Death, appears as a normal human being. He gets more than he bargained for when he visits Earth and falls in love with Miss Mimieux, who plays my daughter."

The veteran performer liked the faster pace of TV filming, the paper reported, "but admits the shooting day is a long one. 'We start an hour earlier than we used to for a motion picture, and we finish an hour or so later. It's wearing, but still better than the stage at my age. Performing eight times a week is just too much—besides, there are no retakes.'"

The Death of Me Yet, October 27, 1971

Cold War drama hits the heartland! Doug McClure is a rural newspaper editor who came to America as a spy for the Russians. Now, one of his former comrades has been sent to kill him. *The Kokomo* (Indiana) *Tribune* called the movie an "Intriguing, suspenseful made-for-TV film. It opens in a typically American community with average people going about their daily business, but we soon discover that the place is actually a detailed reproduction of the community in Russia. Doug McClure, one of the town's citizens, is dispatched to the U.S. as an infiltrator, but he runs away, takes on a new identity, and lives for six years as a happily married newspaper editor. The plot of the tale is picked up here, and it's exciting to see McClure being shadowed by both Russian agents and a determined U.S. intelligence officer (Darren McGavin). Doug McClure is at his best in this film, and the supporting cast, including McGavin, Rosemary Forsyth, and Richard Basehart, is effective."

• A similar plot was used in the execrable 1989 "comedy" *The Experts*, starring John Travolta and Arye Gross. For another village that isn't what it seems to be, see *The People*, on January 22.

A Little Game, October 30, 1971

Just in time for Halloween, a retelling of *The Bad Seed*, the classic 1956 movie about a "perfect" young girl who's not as innocent as she appears—this time with a sex change. Young Mark Gruner didn't kill anyone, did he? After all, it's normal for a kid to be somewhat hostile to a new stepparent (Ed Nelson, who married Gruner's mom, Diane Baker). Things get messy when Nelson starts to suspect the kid *really* doesn't want a new dad. The Appleton, Wisconsin, *Post-Crescent* compared the movie favorably to *The Bad Seed*, calling it a "chilling film," and singled out Gruner, noting the "handsome youngster plays this monster with frightening accuracy." Unlike Patty McCormack, who was Oscar-nominated for the 1956 movie, Gruner did not have much of a (film) career; his résumé lists only a handful of TV and movie parts, with *Jaws 2* as his last role—he played one of police chief Brody's (Roy Scheider) sons.

Two on a Bench, November 2, 1971

Typical Hollywood formula: Put two opposites in the same general space; have them "meet cute"; throw in a few other plot twists and voilà! You have a movie. In this case, a free-spirited woman (Patty Duke) has lunch on a Boston park bench every day, as does a conservative stockbroker (Ted Bessell), but at different times. Unknown to them, the bench is used as a drop-off by spies, and soon this odd couple is on the run.

• Duke and Bessell played opposite each other again in her 1985 sitcom, *Hail to the Chief.* Duke played the first female president, Bessell her astronaut husband. Though it got good reviews for the performers, the show lasted only a season. Two years later, Bessell began directing *The Tracey Ullman Show*, for which he won an Emmy.

• **Spoiler**: The real spy is John Astin, who married Duke the following year.

Revenge!, November 6, 1971

Shelley Winters alert! The film features Winters at her most blowsy and gothic as a grieving mother who wants revenge against the man who "mistreated" her daughter. She gets the man (Bradford Dillman, excellent as always) to her house, according the *Sheboygan* (Wisconsin) *Press*, "by switching briefcases with him … when he shows up for his briefcase, the revenge-bent mother clobbers him over the head, then locks him in a cage in the basement while she plans to dispose of him. Stuart Whitman, playing a psychic, is called in by the missing man's wife to locate him." The *Lowell* (Massachusetts) *Sun* said Winters gives "a tremendous performance." Well … you either love Winters in roles like this or hate her; this is one-third of her 1971 gothic trifecta; the other two are the movies *Who Slew Auntie Roo?* and *What's the Matter with Helen?* Just around the corner was her career-reviving role in *The Poseidon Adventure* (1972).

Do Not Fold, Spindle, or Mutilate, November 9, 1971

Helen Hayes stars with Myrna Loy, Mildred Natwick, and Sylvia Sidney—that's all I need to know to make this a must-watch movie. The plot is cute, but nothing special: Four senior citizens who love to play practical jokes create a fictional woman for a computer dating service, and tire of it as they start to rebuff the respondents. They get their gal "engaged" to end the charade, but it's too late: their "creation" has piqued the interest of a dangerous man. Vince Edwards (Ben Casey) plays the man who makes them regret their prank. Hayes was Emmy-nominated for her role.

Duel, November 13, 1971
Tagline: Fear is the driving force.
Directed by Steven Spielberg, Dennis Weaver stars as a driver harassed by a truck on a long, lonely stretch of road. One of the most terrifying movies ever, and certainly a milestone in TV-movie history, it was written by horror/fantasy vet Richard Matheson. The theme has been redone and reworked ever since its debut. We never actually see the driver of the truck, so the vehicle becomes a stand-in for any kind of malevolence the viewer wants to imprint on it. Spielberg has rarely been better, and certainly never as succinct; his use of camera angles and the handheld camera would be echoed a few years later in his other masterpiece, *Jaws*. The reviews for this were great right out of the box, and the network rushed it onto its TV schedule, knowing it had something good, as a *Movie of the Weekend* (it aired on a Saturday night). The *Anniston* (Alabama) *Star* called *Duel* "a gripping, agonizing tale of suspense, which is essentially Dennis Weaver driving along deserted roads in the high desert country, trying desperately to stay alive: a huge tanker truck, with an unseen driver, is trying to kill him. The story not only sustains itself beautifully, but it also builds to a climax that will leave you limp. It's beautifully photographed, all on location, and the show is heightened by a great soundtrack, which includes Billy Goldenberg's just-right score. ... Mostly it's [just] Dennis, his car and that mean-looking truck. Weaver, like everything else about this fine film, is excellent." The Mansfield, Ohio, *News*

Journal agreed: "All concerned deserve applause as a motoring nightmare that's a highway game of death between a salesman in a compact car and a gasoline truck, sustains its suspense for the full 90 minutes. Salesman Weaver, rolling along on California backroads, can't shake the menacing truck intent on bagging the compact. All attempts to call for help from police and bystanders prove fruitless, and the duel between machine and man turns into a showdown."

• *Duel* merited a brief theatrical release in 1983 with added footage.

• Matheson also wrote the "Prey" segment of another well-known MOTW, *Trilogy of Terror*. See the movie listing in Season Six for more details.

• Weaver was already starring in his hit series *McCloud* when he filmed this MOTW.

Dennis Weaver is having some car, er, truck trouble in Steven Spielberg's *Duel*. Photofest

Mr. and Mrs. Bo Jo Jones, November 16, 1971

Desi Arnaz Jr. once had a promising TV and movie career, but this TV-movie was one of his soggier efforts. Arnaz is a high-school senior who gets his girl (1970s ingénue Christopher Norris) pregnant, feels guilty, and then does the right thing and marries her. When the baby dies, the marriage falls apart, much to the pleasure of the kids' parents, notably Norris' rich, snobby folks, played by Dina Merrill and, of all people, former Fox musical comedy star Dan Dailey! The subject of out-of-wedlock pregnancy remained mostly a network TV taboo even in 1971, but this groundbreaking film, *in that respect only*, was evidence that the times were a changin'. This was way too clichéd and earnest to score. Annoying Tom Bosley is Arnaz's dad, and he appears to be prepping for his whiny, apoplectic performance in *Happy Days*.

The Reluctant Heroes, November 23, 1971

You'll either find this Korean War movie lame or interesting, depending on how you feel about two things: war and Ken Berry. The terminally mild-mannered Berry is a lieutenant put in charge of his soldiers, trapped behind enemy lines, after their captain is killed. But Berry has no combat experience; he's an expert in military history. Natch, he uses his smarts to save the boys. The rest of the cast is solid, though they all play familiar soldier stereotypes: Jim Hutton, Warren Oates, Don Marshall, Soon-Tek Oh as a Korean officer, and, in the odd casting department, Mexican folk singer Trini Lopez as Pvt. Sam Rivera.

The Failing of Raymond, November 27, 1971

Stalker movies were a staple for the MOTW. This one, though the plot is somewhat hackneyed, has two strong lead performances to hold it together. Jane Wyman has one of those roles she could play in her sleep: Mary Bloomquist, a dedicated high school teacher who "faces the greatest teaching challenge of her life." At least, according to ABC's press release. The film opens with Mary, on the eve of her retirement after almost 30 years as a teacher, packing her belongings in class. She's actually several years away from retirement age, but she feels she has nothing more to offer the students. An unhappy love affair with Allan McDonald (Dana Andrews) has added to her malaise, making her unable to teach effectively. Spinster alert! Into the room comes Raymond (Dean Stockwell, also in a role he patented, the seemingly earnest but disturbed young man), who Mary thinks has arrived to help her pack. She has no idea he's a student she failed a decade before, just released from the loony bin. Talk about holding a grudge! Rounding out the great cast are Paul Henreid, Murray Hamilton, and Tim O'Connor.

Brian's Song, November 30, 1971
Tagline: An inspiring true story of friendship and courage.
Directed by Buzz Kulik, based on Gale Sayers' book *I Am Third*. This wonderful but sentimental story about a promising young football player struck down by cancer remains one of the top tearjerkers in any medium, and is often cited (along with *Duel* and *That Certain Summer*) as reasons why the *Movie of the Week* rocked. James Caan gives a very likeable portrayal of the doomed Brian Piccolo, and Billy Dee Williams is stoic, caring, and just about everything you'd want playing his team roommate and best bud Sayers. *Brian's Song* won Emmys in 1972 for Outstanding Single Program, Drama or Comedy, and Outstanding Performance by an Actor in a Supporting Role in Drama, for Jack Warden, who played the no-nonsense but understanding coach of the Chicago Bears, George Halas. It also won the prestigious Peabody Award in

1972. TV veteran Shelley Fabares (who played Donna Reed's daughter in Reed's long-running sitcom) took one of her first grown-up roles as Piccolo's wife. The UPI's Vernon Scott noted the following January, "Once in a great while a movie will be made for television that surpasses the usual B-grade of the genre, much to the astonishment of producers, who would dearly love to release the rarity in theaters. That was the case with *Brian's Song*, which, after its video airing, was shown in theaters." Another thing producers love to do is imitate success by remaking a great film or cribbing its plot. Thus, *Brian's Song* was unnecessarily remade as a TV movie in 2001, with Mekhi Phifer and Sean Maher as Sayers and Piccolo.

The Devil and Miss Sarah, December 4, 1971

Combination Western/horror film stars debonair Gene Barry and sexy 1950s movie and TV starlet Janice Rule as an outlaw (well, the ultimate outlaw, Satan) and Miss Sarah, respectively. The catch here is, Rule and her on-screen hubby (stalwart James Drury) are escorting Barry to justice, but the demon's planning on taking over Miss Sarah's body so he can have sex with her handsome hus ... no, no, no—in order to escape, of course. Drury's extra perceptive, however, and catches on to the demonic plot. Filmed on location in southern Utah.

• Drury was coming off the mammoth success of *The Virginian* (1962-'71, 249 episodes) when he filmed this. His TV co-star, Doug McClure, also found success on a number of MOTWs.

If Tomorrow Comes, December 7, 1971

Sometimes Hollywood throws too much at the audience in an effort to make sure we *get* it; witness this movie, an earnest attempt at a statement on race relations. Patty Duke (once again choosing offbeat material) marries a Japanese man (Frank Liu) on the eve of December 7, 1941. And the movie itself aired on … the 30th anniversary of the attack on Pearl Harbor. Anne Baxter, Pat Hingle, James Whitmore, and Mako, among others, are around to portray varied points of view in a story of prejudice vs. acceptance. *The Lowell* (Massachusetts) *Sun* reviewed the film as "a *Romeo and Juliet* adaptation about a young Japanese-American man and an American girl who marry on Dec. 7. This is a well-intentioned drama which takes a look at the infamous internment of loyal Japanese after the attack on Pearl Harbor. Unfortunately, it is also contrived and slow-moving … with Anne Baxter over-acting the role of a neighbor and confidante of the young marrieds, James Whitmore as Patty's father, and Bennett Ohta and Beulah Quo very good as the boy's parents." On second thought, Anne Baxter overacting is something I'd *pay* to see.

See the Man Run, December 11, 1971

In this odd—or, if you like it, offbeat—kidnap drama, inept kidnappers reach the wrong number, and instead talk to a wannabe actor, who, with his wife, decides to horn in on the ransom money. Of course, some viewers aren't particular, as this review attests: "Stock kidnapping plot undergoes a wrenching, far-out twist. If viewers can accept the contrived premise, they should enjoy it. Linked to a kidnapping through a wrong telephone number, an out-of-work actor decides to cut himself in. Egged on by his wife, the actor discovers his manhood again, running from cops, planning details, and using his acting skills. Robert Culp carries on quite well, with nice assist from Angie Dickinson." Eddie Albert and June Allyson add to the fun.

The Trackers, December 14, 1971

More genre-busting: For most unlikely TV movie pairing ever, I give you … Ernest Borgnine and Sammy Davis Jr. Yes,

McHale and the Candy Man co-star in a Western about a man (Borgnine) whose daughter is kidnapped, so he hires Davis, a tracker (an expert at finding lost people) to save her. It's a drama, it's a comedy, it's about renegade Indians, it's about race relations, its … well, it's an old-fashioned plot filtered through a groovy 1970s lens. Can't we all just get along? Julie Adams, best remembered for her screaming opposite *The Creature from the Black Lagoon* (1954), is Borgnine's wife. Davis co-produced this with Aaron Spelling. John Ford's *The Searchers* was the template for this MOTW; go for the 1956 classic.

What's a Nice Girl Like You…?, December 18, 1971

Great actress Brenda Vaccaro (well, she had a great, sandpapery voice) plays both a working girl and her upper-crust socialite look-alike … and reality just flew out the window! Criminals force the former to impersonate the latter for money. The eclectic cast includes Roddy McDowall, Jo Anne Worley, Jack Warden, and Hollywood vets Vincent Price and Edmond O'Brien, obviously slumming for the paycheck.

• The exact look-alike storyline, in which the same actor or actress plays two different roles who aren't related, or who may be cousins or siblings that just *happen* to have identical looks, is used to death in the soap opera genre. On *All My Children* Kate Collins played the good Natalie and changed into the evil Janet by donning a black wig and glasses. Linda Evans pulled double duty on *Dynasty*, as did Jeanne Cooper on *The Young and the Restless*. The list is endless.

The Astronaut, January 8, 1972

In a plot that resonates of Cold War paranoia, the U.S. government uses plastic surgery to create a double for an astronaut (Monte Markham) who died on the surface of Mars during America's first mission to the red planet. This is done so that the public won't panic, and our space program won't be jettisoned. But will the colonel's wife (Susan Clark) buy the substitute hubby? Written by Harve Bennett, who went on to produce and write several of the best *Star Trek* movies (see also *Death Race* in Season Five). Comparing the film to the classic MOTW *Brian's Song*, Vernon Scott reported in the *Salt Lake City Tribune*, January 8, 1972, "*The Astronaut*, a romantic thriller, stars Jackie Cooper, Monte Markham, Robert Lansing and Susan Clark. Produced at Universal Studios as one of its contracted 90-minute films for ABC, the studio toppers realized too late it had come up with a picture people would pay money to see at the box office. Because the studio is contract-bound to ABC, it cannot pull the film back for bigger profits. It must be shown on the tube."

"I have never had this good a role on television," Markham told Scott. "The story was so good that many additional scenes were made so the picture can be shown as a theatrical release once it has been seen on television." [Just like *Brian's Song*. See November 31, 1971.]

Scott noted Markham had also played two roles in the MOTW *Death Takes a Holiday* (see October 23, 1971), a guest appearance on Sandy Duncan's show, and on his own series, *The Second Hundred Years*. "It's the ultimate ego trip for an actor," Markham said, "especially when he plays a scene with himself. What actor could ask for more? But it can also psych you out because you begin to think in the third person instead of both characters. The trick is to play the two personalities close enough, but not so close as to confuse the audience."

* ***The Night Stalker***, January 11, 1972
* ***The Night Strangler***, January 16, 1973

No one played cynical better than Darren McGavin, and he was in his element as feisty, cynical, abrasive reporter Carl Kolchak, who was stalking a vampire, which in turn was stalking the population of Los Angeles. The wisecracking Kolchak can't get anyone else to believe who's been murdering modern L.A. citizens and draining them of blood, so he takes matters into his own hands. Carol Lynley was Kolchak's understanding babe, a.k.a. the female-in-peril role, something she was adept at playing (see 1964's *Shock Treatment*, 1965's *Bunny Lake Is Missing*, and 1967's *The Shuttered Room*). The initial airing of this MOTW remained in the Top 25 highest-rated movies on television list for many years, with a 33.2 rating and a 54 share.

With such a huge ratings success, Kolchak came back in *Strangler*, this time located in Seattle, chasing an "alchemist" who is killing women because he needs their blood. He's 100 years old, by the way. Almost as good as the first movie, this one benefits from director Dan Curtis' patented atmospheric shots, and a helluva good supporting cast of film and TV character actors, including Al Lewis (as a tramp!), Wally Cox, Margaret Hamilton, John Carradine and Ivor Francis. Additional footage shot but not used featured George "Abner Kravitz" Tobias as an older reporter who'd covered similar homicides in the 1930s. Curtis did not follow star McGavin to the TV series in 1974; quality steadily declined and it was canceled after one year and a season full of sublimely cheesy horror.

• The score is by Bob Cobert, who wrote the music for Curtis' soap opera *Dark Shadows* and other Dan Curtis Productions, such as the movie *Burnt Offerings* (1976) and the TV miniseries *War and Remembrance* (1988).

• "DVD Talk" columnist Bob Gutowski notes, "Vampire Barry Atwater's growls were post-dubbed because the hand-held camera in some shots of him as the undead Janos Skorzeny—who never speaks, which makes him even scarier—was extremely loud in operation."

• There was a book of *The Night Stalker* based on an "unpublished novel" by Jeff Rice, according movie addict Saul Fischer (who copy-edited the first edition of this book). He adds, "There was even a *Night Stalker* fanzine, which I saw about 13 years ago. Chris Carter, who created *The X-Files* has said that *The Night Stalker* was his inspiration. Star McGavin thought the series went in the wrong direction. He felt it should've been more like *The Fugitive*, with Kolchak chasing the undead, as opposed to the 'monster of the week' format."

• As a tribute, Carter created a guest-starring role for McGavin on *The X Files*, retired FBI agent Arthur Dales, in two episodes of the series, in 1998 and 1999.

• *Strangler* co-star Francis was familiar with vampire territory, having played Dr. Franklin on producer Curtis' soap *Dark Shadows*. His daughter is soap actress Genie Francis (*General Hospital's* Laura).

• A new version of the cult series debuted on ABC in the 2005–'06 season, starring Stuart Townsend (masking his Irish accent) as Kolchak, trailing a possibly supernatural foe who's murdered more than once, including Kolchak's wife. This time, the younger, sexier investigator got a skeptical, sexy female reporter counterpart (Gabrielle Union). Ten episodes were filmed. ABC canceled *Night Stalker* after six episodes; then the Sci-Fi Channel picked it up and aired the rest. For fans of the original series, the best moment in the remake came during the pilot episode: Townsend enters the newsroom and says hello to a digitally-inserted image of McGavin.

* **Madame Sin**, January 15, 1972

Bette Davis, after strutting her stuff in a series of gothic murder mysteries on the big screen, continued in full-out camp mode in her small-screen debut. And a camp-feast it is, with Robert Wagner—who, shame on him, also executive-produced—as a CIA agent used as a stooge by the title character (Davis), who's after a nuclear sub. ABC described Madame Sin as, "an all-powerful woman of mystery who, from a remote castle stronghold in Scotland, directs sinister global operations which topple governments and change the course of world history." Come on—this was too far-fetched even for 1972. The press release also claimed that Madame Sin would add "a new dimension to the film career of the two-time Academy Award-winning actress." Hmm. Only if they meant, "Never let this overly hammy broad in front of a camera again." Did I mention that Davis played an Asian woman, and her castle is equipped with all the expected super-villain accoutrements? The latter included a sonic ray that "collapses the brain," and a brain probe machine that can implant thoughts into someone's head. Madame Sin was quite brain-obsessed, it would seem. Audiences in Europe actually *paid* to see this as a theatrical release. This pilot was touted as "a forerunner for a new and dramatic series exploring psychic phenomena and extrasensory perception," but fortunately, never made it to series. Filmed in London and on the Isle of Mull, Scotland. Must have made a nice trip for Ms. Davis.

Getting Away From It All, January 18, 1972

Light comedy about two couples who decide to leave the angst of city life for some country comfort. But of course, another man's grass ain't always greener. This enjoyable trifle is heavy on recognizable TV faces—Larry Hagman, Barbara Feldon, Gary Collins, Vivian Vance, Burgess Meredith, and

Jim Backus. Randy Quaid played one of his first roles in this film, a character named Herbie.

• Vance made a handful of TV and movie appearances after her high-profile roles as Ethel Mertz in *I Love Lucy* (1951-'60, for which she won the first Best Supporting Actress Emmy) and Vivian Bagley on *The Lucy Show* (1962–'65). Though a movie career never developed, she was happier doing stage work and overjoyed to get a commercial (as Maxine, the Maxwell House coffee lady) in the 1970s. "All I wanted after the series was a commercial, because of the money, and being popular got me that…. that's how I've ended up on TV, selling coffee and loving it," she cracked to *Esquire* at the time.

The People, January 22, 1972

Kim Darby plays a teacher who comes to a rural community and eventually discovers the people aren't backward or snooty, they're actually extraterrestrials, trying to hide their "otherness" from the outside world. Racial parable, anyone? Given the times, you can figure out how it ends … on a positive, "We Are the World" note. William Shatner co-stars in one of his early post-*Star Trek* roles, though the plot seems borrowed from his seminal series, or perhaps another of his gigs, *The Twilight Zone*.

• Produced by American Zoetrope, the company founded by Francis Ford Coppola, and executive-produced by Coppola himself.

Women in Chains, January 25, 1972

All-female prison stories have always been a draw, in movies, on stage, in print, or on television. This version has parole officer Lois Nettleton going undercover to investigate brutality in the prison system. So, of course, the only person in the cooler who knows Nettleton's true identity is killed early on, the better for her to endure brutal prison matron Ida Lupino and the ranting of her fellow inmates before the truth is revealed. Jessica Walter, Belinda Montgomery, and Penny Fuller add to the campy fun.

• In an interview with the (Pocatello) *Idaho State Journal* on January 21, a few days before the film aired, the paper pointed out, "The inner workings of women's prisons are no mystery to actress Ida Lupino. Two of her favorite movie roles have been prison officials. Her latest visit to the cell block is *Women in Chains*."

"My first prison film was *Women's Prison* back in 1955," she told the *Journal*. "I was the sadistic warden who was exposed by my husband, Howard Duff, who co-starred with me. I haven't had a part like that until *Women in Chains*. In this drama I play a cruel matron who is finally brought to trial. Roles like this are good for an actress because you can get rid of a lot of frustrations.

"It's sad that so little has been done about prison reform in the years between these pictures. I only hope that after the terrible riot at Attica, public awareness will bring about the reforms that are so desperately needed."

As a director herself, perhaps the preeminent female director of the time, Lupino added, "I believe in the autonomy of the director. There are times when you may want to change something, but usually the director will see what should be done [on his/her own]. We had a fine man in Bernard Kowalski on *Women in Chains*.

"I was flattered, though, that my co-stars Lois Nettleton, Jessica Walter, and Belinda Montgomery, took the trouble to ask my advice about their characterizations. It's not often that that happens."

The MOTW week was a haven for Golden Age Hollywood stars who could still show their chops, like Joseph Cotton, here comforting Olivia De Havilland in *The Screaming Woman* (Season Three). Is she insane or not? The two had answered the same question for Bette Davis in the 1964 big-screen chiller *Hush, Hush Sweet Charlotte*. Photofest

The Screaming Woman, January 29, 1972

Oscar-winning star Olivia de Havilland is not the title screamer, but rather a former mental patient who, upon returning home, hears (or *thinks* she hears) the muffled cries of someone screaming for help, coming from *underground* on her property. Will anyone else believe her? Not for the first three-quarters of the movie, anyway. Her relatives hope this behavior will enable them to put Livvie away and take her money. The combination of a Ray Bradbury story, de Havilland at her emotive best, and excellent support from Joseph Cotten, Laraine Stephens, Walter Pidgeon, and Ed Nelson, add up to a classic thriller. This MOTW was shot in Technicolor, which was unique for a TV movie of this era. Cotten and de Havilland also co-starred on the big screen in *Airport '77*.

Hardcase, February 1, 1972

What would you do if your wife abandoned home and hearth and took up with a Mexican revolutionary? If she was sexy Stefanie Powers and you were rock-solid Clint Walker, you'd go after her. Walker is a soldier-of-fortune who returns to his Texas ranch to find it has been sold and Powers is gone, baby, gone. Cartoon empire Hanna-Barbera produced, an unusual effort for the company most associated with producing some of the best-known and most popular cartoon characters of all time, such as *The Flintstones*, *The Jetsons*, *Yogi Bear*, and *Huckleberry Hound*.

When Michael Calls, February 5, 1972

Our heroine (Elizabeth Ashley) starts receiving phone calls from her 15-years-dead nephew. Is she going nuts? Is someone trying to *Gaslight* her? This one lives up to ABC's hype: "*When Michael Calls* is a nightmarish drama about a woman terrorized by phone calls from a child, presumably dead, but determined to avenge his mother's death. The ringing of a telephone becomes a living hell for Helen Connelly (Elizabeth Ashley). Each time she picks up the receiver, a child's voice pleads, 'Auntie-my-Helen. Find me! Stop me! Help me!' It is the tortured voice of her nephew Michael. Years before, when Helen reluctantly committed her sister, Michael's insane mother, to a mental institution, the boy ran away. Later he was presumed to have died from exposure in a blizzard."

The only time you really don't expect to hear from family is when they're, um, dead … which is why Elizabeth Ashley can't decide whether to answer the phone *When Michael Calls*. Photofest

Helen asks her ex-husband (Ben Gazzara, *The Fugitive*) for help. Also helping out (or is he?) is Michael's brother, Craig (Michael Douglas, soon to start his march toward fame on *The Streets of San Francisco*), who is the director of a school for disturbed boys (potential crazy person alert!). Everyone begins to think the calls are coming from a sick student at Douglas' school, and then things turn murderous. First, one of Helen's friends dies a horrible death, then the sheriff (Al Waxman, *Cagney & Lacey*). ABC noted in its press release. "Helen begins to suspect that the deaths are linked to some terrible event in the distant past." ... You mean, worse than her sister going insane and her nephew disappearing and presumably dying?! This MOTW terrified me when it first aired.

• Based on the book by John Farris, who also penned *The Fury*, in which psychic kids become government pawns. It was filmed by Brian DePalma in 1978.

Second Chance, February 8, 1972

Geoff Smith (*Family Affair*'s Brian Keith) is tired. He's a successful stockbroker, but he has an ulcer, sees a shrink, and is generally unhappy. What to do? Why, buy a ghost town he noticed for sale in Nevada, and make it a haven for those who want another chance at life. That's what I'd do. Wouldn't you? Our heroine (Elizabeth Ashley in a rare double play—starring in two MOTWs within one week) this time helps hubby Smith run the town he's named—just in case you didn't get it—Second Chance. TV staples Pat Carroll (*Caesar's Hour*, *Make Room for Daddy*), Kenneth Mars (*The Little Mermaid*, *Malcolm in the Middle*), Avery Schreiber (*My Mother, The Car*), Ann Morgan Guilbert (*The Dick Van Dyke Show*, *The Nanny*), and William Windom (*The Farmer's Daughter*, *Murder She Wrote*) were residents vying for another try at making their town work, while Rosie Grier and Emily Yancy added the requisite racial drama to the equation. If this had gone to series, the show would've focused on those who came to town looking for ... yup, a second chance.

Hound of the Baskervilles, February 9, 1972

The sounds you hear are the hounds wailing at what a disaster this movie is, from taking liberties with perhaps the most well-known Sherlock Holmes tale of all, to the fish-out-of-water casting of Americans like William Shatner and Anthony Zerbe. Bernard Fox (*Bewitched*'s Dr. Bombay) is the only bright spot, as Dr. Watson. Look for the 1939 Basil Rathbone-Nigel Bruce classic instead. First of three pilots for a proposed series called *Great Detectives*. (See also *A Very Missing Person* on March 4.)

Call Her Mom, February 15, 1972

Some great comic actors perk up this sitcom of a movie about a "sexy waitress" (lovable Connie Stevens) who becomes the house mother for a fraternity. It was directed by Jerry Paris, and featured Gloria DeHaven, Jim Hutton, Van Johnson, Corbett Monica, Kathleen Freeman, and Charles Nelson Reilly (his most memorable line: "She's not a house mother—she's a house tootsie!"). Gail Parent wrote the script; she penned the best-selling book *Sheila Levine Is Dead and Living in New York* in 1972. Stevens was rewarded with this pilot when her 1970-'71 season sitcom pilot went bust. This one didn't sell, either.

• Ross Bagdasarian created the original music for this film; he also created Alvin and the Chipmunks, and sang on the group's evergreen holiday hit, "The Chipmunk Song (Christmas Don't Be Late)."

Kung Fu, February 22, 1972

Circa 1800: a Shaolin monk, part American, part Asian, fights evil and rights wrongs in America, after fleeing China upon avenging his teacher's death (he's being pursued by Chinese bounty hunters). David Carradine became a star as the monk in question, a role originally intended for Hong Kong legend Bruce Lee. Fortunately, for the three-year series that followed this pilot (1972–'75), Carradine underplayed, which worked well in capturing an Asian mystique as well as the moodiness of his character. The fight scenes were not as over-the-top as in the kung-fu movies of the same period, and the show even preached non-violence on occasion.

• An interview in the *The Robesonian*, (Lumberton, N.C.) August 6, 1972—coinciding with a repeat of the MOTW before the series began in October—noted, "If awards were given out to actors who continually play unusual roles, David Carradine would be a perennial nominee. The son of veteran actor John Carradine has built his career around his ability to portray strange and often bizarre characters.

"Carradine will be seen in still another unusual portrayal when he stars in *Kung Fu*, a unique western drama on ABC [portraying] a Chinese-American fugitive from a murder charge in Imperial China. Working on the transcontinental railroad in the 1860's, he uses his knowledge of the ancient art of personal combat, kung fu, to help the coolies laboring on the railroad overcome wretched working conditions."

"I feel this is the best part I've ever had. In fact, it's not like anything I have ever seen done on film," Carradine told the paper. "The man I play uses [his tangible] mental strength to become what I like to call a humble hero. It was a difficult character to learn because I was so unfamiliar with the art of kung fu and its background. But we had a brilliant technical advisor in David Chow, a world renowned expert on the subject."

Kung Fu did preclude the actor from playing a certain type of role: "I had to have my head completely shaved for the film—which means that unless I get a wig there won't be any hippies in my acting future for a while…." Good thing he already played one in the MOTW *Maybe I'll be Home in the Spring* (See Season Two).

**Two for the Money*, February 26, 1972

Two cops (the black and white team of Robert Hooks and Stephen Brooks) quit the force to become private eyes and solve a case that's remained opened for 10 years involving a missing man wanted for five murders. The man's sister wants to find him because their mother is dying, and Walter Brennan wants revenge for his family. A great supporting cast helps this tight little detective yarn, including Shelley Fabares (*The Donna Reed Show, Coach*), Catherine Burns, and Oscar winners Anne Revere, Richard Dreyfuss, and Mercedes McCambridge. An Aaron Spelling pilot that didn't sell.

**The Eyes of Charles Sand*, February 29, 1972

Shades of *The Eyes of Laura Mars*. In that 1978 movie, Faye Dunaway gets to see a killer performing his evil deeds as they happen, through his eyes. In this MOTW, Peter Haskell has inherited the psychic ability to see things that he shouldn't be able to see—like the past, the future, and people who have passed on. Though he doesn't see events in sharp focus, he does help a woman whose brother may have been murdered. A typically solid MOTW week supporting cast is featured in this failed Warner Bros. pilot, including Joan Bennett, Adam (*Batman*) West, Bradford Dillman, Sharon Farrell, and Barbara Rush.

• An uncredited Henry Mancini did the music. According to the book *Unsold Television Pilots*, "A composer's strike prevented Warner Bros. from commissioning an original score, and instead they pirated Mancini's soundtrack from *Wait Until Dark*."

*A Very Missing Person, March 4, 1972

Perhaps this should be called *Murder, She* Almost *Wrote*. Eve Arden stars as former teacher Hildegarde Withers who tries to help the police find a missing heiress. Arden is wonderful as always, and ably supported by James Gregory and Julie Newmar, but as a mystery, this MOTW was a tad too tame. Hildegarde was played in several 1930s films by character actresses ZaSu Pitts and Edna May Oliver.

• This was the second pilot for a proposed Universal TV series called *Great Detectives*, which would have featured three different sleuths in rotating dramas. The first was the MOTW *The Hound of the Baskervilles* (see February 9). The third— 1972's *The Adventures of Nick Carter*, starring Robert Conrad as a private detective at the turn of the 20th century, not too far removed from his *The Wild Wild West* territory—was not part of the MOTW series.

• Harold Schindler, television editor of the *Salt Lake (City) Tribune*, added, in his February 17, 1972 column, that in the early days of television no comediennes "were as lofty in the public eye as the late Joan Davis, the ubiquitous Lucille Ball, and straight-faced, wise-cracking Eve Arden. Lucy refused to give up her [grip] on network television and became an institution; Miss Arden retired…. Perhaps this will mark the return of a delightfully entertaining actress to a medium which sorely needs her talent."

Yes, Arden was a rare commodity, and yes, she was well remembered as Connie Brooks long after the show ended (and still is). But unfortunately, this pilot never sold. And Schindler apparently forgot Arden's two years on the sitcom *The Mothers-in-Law* (1967-'69), plus a score or more of other TV and movie appearances after *Our Miss Brooks* ended in 1956 (including one season of *The Eve Arden Show* in 1957-'58).

Her greatest late-career triumph came in the 1978 blockbuster *Grease*, playing the wisecracking Principal McGee.

* *The Rookies*, March 7, 1972

Starring Georg Stanford Brown, Sam Melville, Michael Ontkean, and Jennifer Billingsley (whose role in the subsequent series went to future *Charlie's Angel* Kate Jackson), this MOTW gave birth to one of the first of the network "supercop" shows (running from 1972–'76). The more realistic, darker shows that followed (*Hill Street Blues*, *NYPD Blue*, the *C.S.I.* and *Law and Order* franchises) make *The Rookies* look tame now, but it did routinely tackle the top social issues of its day. The crusty Gerald S. O'Loughlin replaced Sergeant Darren McGavin in the series, and Tyne Daly, then wife of co-star Brown (also sister of Tim Daly and daughter of *Medical Center*'s James Daly), had a recurring role, long before she played Mary Beth Lacey. The TV movie and series (1972-'76) were produced by Aaron Spelling.

• In an interview in the *Burlington* (N.C.) *Times-News*, Saturday, March 4, 1972, Joan Crosby noted that McGavin "has done guest appearances on several series and made a pilot for NBC and Warner Brothers called *Father on Trial* (a.k.a. *Here Comes the Judge*), costarring Barbara Feldon. The pilot is a comedy, something Darren wants to do, after years in heavy drama or cop shows."

"No more cops and robbers series for me. I've turned down four this year," McGavin told Crosby. "Search and seek, that's all it is today. Everybody's a private detective: doctors are private detectives, lawyers are private detectives, and private detectives are private detectives. Look at the plot structure of the stories you see on TV: they're all detective stories."

"*The Rookies* is a pilot," Crosby continued, "but not for McGavin. It's the second Aaron Spelling production he has done this year [*The Death of Me Ye*t was the other one; see October 27], and he smiles and says, 'I told Aaron forthrightly on the set that I have done him two favors this year and now he owes me a favor: the best possible script. After a few years in this business, you get an objective sense of oneself. I read *The Rookies* and said, 'Yeah, they need me.''

McGavin did go to series as Carl Kolchak, based on his *Night Stalker* MOTWs (see January 11), and he did a lot of detective work on the show, but he was technically playing a reporter. He finally got his hit sitcom in a recurring role as *Murphy Brown*'s dad, for four episodes that aired 1989-'92.

Season Four: 1972–1973

The Longest Night, September 12, 1972
This tense kidnapping drama boasts solid actors David Janssen and James Farentino. The story is one that Hollywood keeps mining: a woman is kidnapped and buried underground in a coffin while police try to find her. Used in a 2005 episode of the spy series *Alias*, in which heroine Sydney (Jennifer Garner), is the victim, but also redone as a TV movie in 1990: *83 Hours 'Til Dawn*. Not to mention being a major plot point in the Dutch film *The Vanishing* (1988) and its American remake (1993). And … the popular forensic show *C.S.I.* had one of its (male) detectives imprisoned by a serial killer in a coffin-like tomb in the cliff-hanger season five finale (May 2005).
• Co-stars Phyllis Thaxter and Skye Aubrey were real-life mother and daughter; Aubrey is the daughter of Thaxter and former CBS president James Aubrey.

* ***The Daughters of Joshua Cabe***, September 13, 1972
* ***The Daughters of Joshua Cabe Return***, January 28, 1975
* ***The New Daughters of Joshua Cabe***, May 29, 1976
Buddy Ebsen starred in this genial MOTW as a fur trapper who, trying to keep his land in the face of homesteading laws, hires three not-so-perfect beauties (a hooker, a thief, and a convict) to pose as his daughters. With charming Lesley Ann Warren, Karen Valentine, and Sandra Dee playing the daughters, the movie was a great success. Still, nobody clamored for them as a series or to *Return*, but they did anyway, in a totally recast

and much less charming sequel, with Dan Dailey replacing Ebsen and unknowns—except for Brooke Adams, subbing for Warren—as the titular ladies. A kidnap plot was thrown in for good measure. Finally, *The New Daughters of Joshua Cabe* actually featured even lesser-known actresses as the daughters. John McIntyre took over as Cabe, now a part-time sheriff accused of murder. It was not officially part of the MOTW series since it aired a year after the series ended. All three were produced by the ubiquitous Aaron Spelling.

The Daughters of Joshua Cabe (Buddy Ebsen) were two Gidgets (small-screen Gidget Karen Valentine, bottom left, and big-screen Gidget Sandra Dee, right) and one Cinderella (Lesley Ann Warren, top left, who played Cindy in Rodgers & Hammerstein's 1965 TV version). Photofest

• The first *Joshua Cabe* marked one of the few adult roles for former teen star Sandra Dee. Forever typecast as teens Gidget and Tammy in theatrical movies, Dee virtually disappeared from acting in the late 1960s after her divorce from singer Bobby Darin. It's a shame, because her genuinely sweet personality also shone through in dramas such as 1959's *Imitation of Life* and 1960's *Portrait in Black*, as well as lighter fare like *Cabe*. Dee passed away in February 2005 from kidney disease.

No Place to Run, September 19, 1972

A boy's (Scott Jacoby) adoptive parents die, so he runs off to Canada with grandpa (Herschel Bernardi) in order to escape being raised by the state. "*No Place To Run* is a nice film," wrote *The Edwardsville* (Illinois) *Intelligencer*, "not great, but good and a change of pace [from] the action shows [that abound]. [Jacoby] is the adopted son of Bernardi's children, dead a year when this opens. Bernardi has neglected to notify the authorities, and now they feel the old man isn't able to care for the lad. The tale builds on the relationship between these two, strong enough to force the old gentleman into a foolhardy action to preserve it. Larry Hagman, Stefanie Powers, Neville Brand, Kay Medford and Tom Bosley also appear, but their roles are minor. The story belongs to Bernardi and Jacobi and they carry it very well."

Haunts of the Very Rich, September 20, 1972

Atmosphere is key to a horror or fantasy film, and this movie had it in spades. A collection of different character types—played by TV and movie veterans like Ed Asner, Cloris Leachman, Anne Francis, and Robert Reed—are on a plane, heading, we think, to an exotic vacation spot. But this is not the pilot for *The Love Boat*; it's more like an early trip to *Fantasy Island*, except all the fantasies are dark and gruesome. Each passenger is hiding a secret: Francis is a pill-popping housewife, Reed a conflicted minister, and so on. They arrive, and are shepherded by the imposing Moses Gunn to their quarters. That's when they begin to

MOTW damsel in distress Cloris Leachman huddles with Lloyd Bridges in an attempt to figure out just where the, er, *hell* they went on vacation in *Haunts of the Very Rich*. Photofest

understand they're not on vacation ... and they might be way past the point of caring. Similar plots have made it to the big screen—*Outward Bound* (1930) and *Between Two Worlds* (1944) come to mind—but few are as tight and taut as this one.

• Contributing greatly to the aura of mystery is the location shooting at Villa Vizcaya, a former private winter retreat now open to the public as a museum. The main building, designed after the Italian Renaissance and built on Florida's Biscayne Bay, was begun in 1916 and took two years to finish.

The gardens are magnificent and very expansive, and that's where you see the guests in this movie milling about, having cocktails, and searching for answers. I visited Vizcaya in 1988, and remember it feeling very familiar. After a second glance at this movie on late-night TV, I knew why.

Moon of the Wolf, September 26, 1972

Louisiana Sheriff David Janssen has his hands full when it begins to appear that a werewolf is responsible for murders in his sleepy Southern town. *The Hollywood Reporter* called this, "a fascinating modern-day reworking of the werewolf myth which was filmed on location in primeval Louisiana swamps and is better written, better acted, and more genuinely suspenseful than the rash of feature fright pieces which have long since replaced legitimate horror with grisly bloodletting." Others found the movie concentrated too much on a rekindled romance plot and not enough on the werewolf. So there! With Barbara Rush, Bradford Dillman, and *General Hospital*'s John Beradino, who plays a doctor who had an affair with the first werewolf victim.

• Beradino also famously played a physician on *GH* for 33 years, Dr. Steve Hardy. His unique career featured a long stretch in major league baseball, playing from 1939-'53, with three years out while he served during WWII. He was on the Cleveland Indians when the team won the World Series in 1948.

Say Goodbye, Maggie Cole, September 27, 1972

Lots of A-list classic Hollywood actresses found new lives in TV movies, and Susan Hayward was no exception. Though she came late to the game, she did make this and another TV movie in 1972 (*Heart of Anger*, in which she played a lawyer). One might wish for a less sentimental treatment of the subject matter, but Hayward gives her all to the part of a widowed,

caring doctor who is convinced by colleague Darren McGavin to treat patients in an inner-city (read: ghetto) medical clinic.
• The title song, "Learn to Say Goodbye," is sung by the great Dusty Springfield.
• Other than a cameo in the 1972 Western *The Revengers*, *Maggie Cole* would prove to be Hayward's final role. Her last public appearance came as a presenter at the 1974 Academy Awards.

Playmates, October 3, 1972

A lawyer (Alan Alda) and a welder (Doug McClure) meet cute through their kids at Kiddieland—no, this isn't a gay romance; it's still 1972 and *Will & Grace* is long way off; see *That Certain Summer* (November 1, 1972) for a serious treatment of a gay relationship. They are both newly divorced and seem to have little else in common, yet they develop a friendship over tales of marital woe. Once their sons become friends, the two dads see each other regularly at play dates, and, curious about each others' wives (Barbara Feldon and Connie Stevens, respectively), scheme to meet them. Unexpectedly, romance occurs with the newly paired couples, causing all kinds of complications, good and bad. Though this might seem like just a silly comedy, it actually has some heart, due to the actors involved; the *Lowell* (Massachusetts) *Sun* said the film had "an honest script, with real characters." The always-watchable Eileen Brennan has a small role.
• The *Sun* noted at the end of its review, as an afterthought: "Oh, a nude painting of McClure is seen." That was reason enough to keep *me* watching.

Rolling Man, October 4, 1972

Dennis Weaver's in prison for four years; his wife kicks the bucket and their two sons disappear. When he's released, he goes after his kids. The *Charleston* (West Virginia) *Gazette* noted, "Weaver plays a born-loser, wandering about the country after serving a prison term, looking for his sons, and dreaming of becoming a successful race track driver [!!]. The drama is uneven and may test a viewer's patience, but it is filled with an uncompromising sense of reality. Prison sequences, sleazy bars, and small town auto tracks form the sordid background for a colorful collection of characters the man encounters along the way. Given material with a sense of pathos, Weaver registers with impact, and so do Sheree North, Don Stroud, and particularly Jimmy Dean, as a fast-talking operator Weaver meets in jail." The great supporting cast also includes Donna Mills, Slim Pickens, and Agnes Moorehead as Grandmother.

Night of Terror, October 10, 1972

A schoolteacher is pursued by a killer who wants her to forget about a murder she witnessed ... forget *permanently*. According to *The New York Times*, "It took several years and several TV movies like *Night of Terror* for Donna Mills to outgrow her 'woman in jeopardy' period. Here she is pursued by a syndicate hit man. Mills doesn't know why, but she does know that her stalker has already killed two people in order to get to her. The lynchpin of the mystery is an earlier traumatic experience which Mills has blocked from her memory." The cast is a weird but interesting mix, including Martin Balsam, Catherine Burns, Chuck Connors, and Agnes Moorehead as "Bronsky."

• Eddie Egan, the ex-cop who was the model for Gene Hackman's Popeye Doyle in *The French Connection*, has a small role as, what else, a cop.

• This was Moorehead's final appearance in the MOTW series. She had finished her long run on *Bewitched* the previous season, and died in 1974 at the age of 73.

Lt. Schuster's Wife, October 11, 1972

The capable title character, played by Lee Grant, is out to prove her late husband (Paul Burke), a cop, wasn't on the take after he's threatened while on an important case, and then ambushed and shot. Jack Warden (an Emmy winner for the MOTW *Brian's Song*), is Schuster's captain, and Don Galloway (*Ironside*) his younger partner, with Eartha Kitt (*Batman*'s Catwoman) in a cameo as "Lady." Meooooooow!

Goodnight, My Love, October 17, 1972

This missing-persons yarn is set in 1940s Los Angeles, an homage to any number of Raymond Chandler novels (and check out the Chandleresque title). Richard Boone is a private eye, down on his luck, Michael Dunn his diminutive assistant, Barbara Bain takes the Mary Astor role, and Victor Buono does his best Sydney Greenstreet impersonation in this combination murder mystery/camp-fest. Written and directed with zest and obvious fondness for the genre by Peter Hyams, the plot has something to do with Bain's character's brother having gone missing, but it's really not about that, of course. Just enjoy the ride.

• The classic Hollywood playground of the stars, Ciro's on Sunset Boulevard, was used for Buono's nightclub's interiors and exteriors. The former nightclub, which became a rock venue in the 1960s, is now the site of the Comedy Store, which opened there in 1972.

A Great American Tragedy, October 18, 1972

VHS tagline: He lost his job and his sanity!

This is a tragedy that most of us can identify with—losing your job. It happens to middle-aged George Kennedy and his life falls apart. Vera Miles plays his wife. The *Mansfield* (Ohio) *News Journal* reported, "Don't miss this topical story about a successful aerospace engineer whose life undergoes a complete reversal when he's fired from the job he has held for 20 years. This modern-day dilemma has been explored in documentaries but, somehow, the personal dramatic treatment it receives here really drives the facts home. George Kennedy and Vera Miles are excellent as the couple who face unexpected struggles and challenges when their affluent world crumbles, and the script by Caryl Ledner is adult, believable and affecting." Unfortunately, this MOTW is, if anything, even more relevant today.

• James Woods has a small supporting role, but is listed as a co-star and pictured on the VHS box cover to capitalize on his later fame.

George Kennedy takes time out for a cold one with wife Vera Miles as he figures out what to do with his life in *A Great American Tragedy*. **Photofest**

Short Walk to Daylight, October 24, 1972

Way before Sylvester Stallone flexed his muscles rescuing people trapped in the Lincoln Tunnel in 1996's *Daylight* came this MOTW featuring a varied group of people trapped in the New York subways after an earthquake. James Brolin and *Ironside*'s Don Mitchell are the only "names" in this cast, but this MOTW got about as much respect from the critics as Sly's later effort, which is to say, none. Here's a snip from the *Williamstown* (Massachusetts) *Transcript*: "*Short Walk to Daylight* is hysterical, loud, frenetic and filled with unbelievable contrivances. Basically eight characters, seven of them clichéd, are in the subway in the early hours of a Sunday morning, en route home to Brooklyn. A devastating earthquake hits and they attempt to find their way through the rubble to safely. Only the subway conductor, played by James McEachin is believable, although Abbey Lincoln as a concerned black mother and Suzanne Charney as a lonely girl with a sense of humor manage to bring a few good moments to their roles."

Family Flight, October 25, 1972

When a plane crashes in the Mexican desert, tensions between family members get in the way of finding a solution to their problem. Rod Taylor is the solid-as-a-rock dad, Dina Merrill his alcoholic wife, and Kristoffer Tabori their son, who's returned home after 18 months away with his daughter. The four fractured psyches get on a plane and head for Baja. A crash landing leads to a desperate search for a way out. Good acting keeps this one from falling into familiar clichés.

• The movie's climax was filmed with the cooperation of the U. S. Navy, using the carrier *USS Ranger*.

• Sandbagged: *The Bee* (Danville Va.) interviewed Taylor and noted he was "back in the sand again for filming of *Family*

Flight, despite a promise to himself never to do another desert picture. The main setting of the film is an isolated desert area. 'The year before, I'd done a series, *The Bearcats*, which filmed on location in Arizona and New Mexico,' the rugged actor explained. 'Then I went to the Mexican desert for a John Wayne film with Ann-Margret. It was hot and grubby, and I vowed no more desert pictures. Then, after I had been back in Hollywood only two weeks, the offer came to do *The Heroes* with Rod Steiger, and I couldn't afford to turn it down even though it meant shooting on the Sahara.'

"When Taylor returned to Hollywood and was asked to star with Merrill and Tabori in *Flight*, he reasoned, 'Only three days of the movie were to be filmed on the desert, in the Apple Valley area of California. Besides, it would mean a reunion for Dina and me—we'd worked together in 1960 in an episode of *Hong Kong*, my first fling in a TV series.'"

The Bounty Man, October 31, 1972

Not Nancy Walker's male paper towel counterpart, but rather, hunky Clint Walker, who goes after his wife's killer and, on a tip, finds an isolated almost-ghost town filled with wanted criminals, including his quarry, John Ericson (*Honey West*). But Walker finds himself falling for Margot Kidder, playing Ericson's gal-pal in this Western, who insists on coming along as Walker brings Ericson to justice. Sturdy effort with two strapping male stars.

That Certain Summer, November 1, 1972

Ad Tagline: Homosexuality is something people never talk about. If they did, this family would never have to face …
That Certain Summer.
A landmark television movie—actually, a landmark movie, period—this was the first major American film to deal with homosexuality in a non-prejudiced way. The swinging '60s and

receptive '70s had paved the way for a flick like this, in which sensitive teen Scott Jacoby reacts to his divorced dad's (Hal Holbrook) relationship with—wait for it—a MAN (Martin Sheen, no less, in an early role). Hope Lange is Holbrook's ex-wife, who married him knowing he was gay but thought she could change him. The ending is bittersweet, and nothing is totally resolved—just like real life, eh? The American Psychiatric Association declared that homosexuality was not an illness the following year; this movie opened the dialogue for Americans to begin understanding, or at least discussing, the once-taboo subject. Underplayed to perfection by its top-notch cast (Jacoby won an Emmy), *That Certain Summer* still speaks to all of us about accepting your loved ones for who they are, and what the real definition of "normal" is.

Hal Holbrook (left) is a gay man trying to figure out how to tell his son (Emmy winner Scott Jacoby) about his lover, Martin Sheen, during *That Certain Summer*. A revolutionary movie for *any* week in the early 1970s. Photofest

• In *TV Guide*'s "Close-Up" look at the movie in that week's edition, the editors began with this: "Television grows up a little with this groundbreaking—and adult—drama."

• Jacoby's wordy Emmy category—Outstanding Performance by an Actor in a Supporting Role in Drama, a Continuing or One-Time Appearance in a Series, or for a Special Program—disappeared shortly thereafter; it pitted series regulars, MOTW guest stars, and performers in dramatic specials against each other, which wasn't quite equitable of the Television Academy. As of this writing, statuettes are awarded for lead and supporting actor/actress in drama and comedy series, and mini-series or specials; guest actor and actress in drama and comedy series; and individual performance in variety or music programming.

• Picture this: a small town boy, growing up closeted and gay and teased nearly to death in a suffocating, small-minded borough (it wasn't even big enough to be a town!) in New Jersey. When I saw this movie, I was already a sophomore in college and had just finished seeing a shrink at the behest of my folks. (I realized he would be of no help to me when he advised me that if I wanted to be straight, all I needed to do was screw a woman.) Mmm-hmm. All I *really* needed to do was stop seeing him, and work it out on my own. Then, this MOTW came on the air, and all of a sudden I had a positive view of my gayness—a major medium had validated who I was for the first time. I was at a liberal school and my (all-male) dorm mates could've care less about my sexuality. But it's impossible to overestimate how positively *That Certain Summer* affected me (and, I'm sure, many other gay viewers).

The Crooked Hearts, November 8, 1972

The still-debonair Douglas Fairbanks Jr. co-stars with the ever-delectable Roz Russell (in her final role) in a comedy-mystery about a group of disappearing senior citizens. As might be expected, *The Lowell* (Massachusetts) *Sun* noted that this crime caper was "lifted above the average by the presence of Rosalind Russell, in a beautiful performance, Douglas Fairbanks, still the most impeccable charmer around, and Maureen O'Sullivan, as beautiful as ever. They are in a tale that is part Medicare love story and part a great cheating cheaters kind of game. Ross Martin plays a detective with Michael Murphy as a young legman … working on the case of five missing ladies, all elderly, all with money and all having possibly joined a lonely-hearts club: Is Rosalind, obviously a distinguished and wealthy widow, the next victim? Or is she something else? And what about that charmer Fairbanks plays? And who is that rugged athlete played by Kent Smith? These old pros are so good it's too bad the story didn't stay filled with surprises. It's highly predictable in the wrap-up."

The Victim, November 14, 1972

VHS Tagline: The phone isn't the only thing that's dead in Susan's house.

Elizabeth Montgomery must have been itching to get away from light comedy. In fact, after *Bewitched*, she never played a comedic role again. But why she picked this formulaic thriller as her first role after finishing up *Bewitched* remains a bigger mystery than anything in the film. Liz is penned up in a house during a bad electrical storm (no phone, etc.). She's come to support her soon-to-be divorced sister, who is already dead. Will Liz be next? Snippy housekeeper Eileen Heckart is the only one who shows signs of life. Vapid George Maharis portrays sis' husband. Are either the killer? Is some else? Does anyone care? Montgomery spent a large portion of her post-*Bewitched* TV career in films about women victimized by crazed male assailants.

• Montgomery played opposite a future real-life alleged "crazed male assailant" in the 1977 TV movie *A Killing Affair*, but they were portraying two police officers having an affair. Still, *The Abilene* (Texas) *Reporter-News* story about the film is too scarily ironic not to note. So here goes:

"Last spring Elizabeth Montgomery was visiting the Renaissance Faire in the San Fernando valley when a middle-aged woman approached her. She was a fan of *Bewitched* and she asked what the actress was working in. 'I'm doing a television movie with O.J. Simpson,' Miss Montgomery replied. 'Such a nice person,' said the woman. 'Yes, it's a love story between two police detectives,' the actress remarked.

"The woman's face went blank. 'You. O.J. Simpson. A love story? Well!' She stalked back into the crowd. Elizabeth Montgomery is prepared for such reactions when she and the football and TV commercial star appear in *A Killing Affair* on CBS Sept. 21. Not only do they fall in love while investigating a case together; his character of Woodrow York happens to be married.

"Oh, I'm sure I'll be getting hate mail, and I don't care," said Miss Montgomery. "Both O.J. and I realized we would get a strong reaction from the show, but we went ahead and did it. I think it's a good show, though I hate the title." One final irony: the review of the movie, next to the Montgomery interview, was headlined: "O.J. Simpson Effective in *Killing Affair.*"

* ***All My Darling Daughters***, November 22, 1972
* ***My Darling Daughters' Anniversary***, November 7, 1973
The first *Daughters* movie is a dramedy about a widowed judge (Robert Young) who has to supervise his four daughters' weddings, all on the same day (and in a leftover 1960s plot complication, three of the grooms are of different religions—

Jewish, Presbyterian, Zen Buddhist—and the fourth is an atheist). The only smart thing he does is to hire sassy Eve Arden as the wedding coordinator. Sharon Gless plays the feminist daughter in an early role. Yes, it was sappy, but that's what we used to call "heartwarming" during the Vietnam War era. It spawned a treacly sequel, in which Young gives his daughters an anniversary present: *He's* getting remarried! Imagine the antics. Unfortunately, Eve Arden is not his intended. That was Ruth Hussey.

• *Dark Shadows* star Lara Parker replaced Fawne Harriman as one of the darling daughters, Charlotte, in the sequel. Harriman later starred in another soap, *Somerset*.

Home for the Holidays, November 28, 1972

Tagline: There's nothing more chilling … than a warm family gathering!

This was not your typical family gathering. An all-star cast enacts a scary, suspenseful tale about a father (Walter Brennan, in one of his final film appearances) who asks his four estranged daughters home for Christmas to help prove that his new wife is trying to kill him. Eleanor Parker plays the oldest daughter, Alex, a neurotic mess; Jessica Walter is Freddie, a drug-addicted mess still mourning her mother's death after more than a decade; Jill Haworth is Jo, a mess at marriage; and Sally Field, pre-movie career, is Christine, the baby (a student mess-in-training). Julie Harris, playing against type, is the potentially poisonous bride, creepily humming "Silent Night" during a vicious (and loud) storm. It's possible that she killed her first husband. And then there's *someone* outside—we only know he/she is wearing a hooded yellow slicker, carrying a pitchfork, and wearing red gloves. The gloves, by the way, are seen on the hands of various characters inside the house throughout the movie. Once the storm hits, isolating the family in the house, the fun, and murders, begin. It's a real treat to watch the actresses sink their teeth into this tasty whodunnit. There's sibling rivalry, madness, drugs, sex, and murder; what more could one ask for in a gothic thriller?

• The script was by Joseph Stefano, who did similar duty on Alfred Hitchcock's *Psycho*, so he knew a few things about suspense.

• The house in this movie was used earlier in the MOTW *Crowhaven Farm* (see Season Two).

• Field and Parker played an estranged mother and daughter in the earlier MOTW, *Maybe I'll Come Home in the Spring*.

Eleanor Parker, Sally Field and Jill Haworth are three of four sisters (!)—Jessica Walter is not pictured—who are beginning to realize that maybe it wasn't a smart idea to come *Home for the Holidays*. **Photofest**

The Heist, November 29, 1972

The wrong man is made to appear guilty in this crime drama: Christopher George is an armored car guard forced to participate in a robbery by a gang of four (including *Three's Company*'s Norman Fell!) who convince him they've kidnapped his daughter. Turns out that wasn't true, and now cynical detective Howard Duff believes George is just making the whole thing up. But the gang is watching him as he tries to prove his innocence, and thwarting George at every turn. Elizabeth Ashley is his supportive wife. Well-acted caper film.

The Couple Takes a Wife, December 5, 1972

Comedy in which Bill Bixby and Paula Prentiss, both career-oriented and neither wanting to give that up, decide they need another woman around the house when their maid quits. The solution is to hire Valerie Perrine, who looks like a movie star but cleans house like a champ (that always happens). Comic complications arise, natch, when hubby has to go on vacation with the kids and housekeeper, but the wife is delayed. Since this is the 1970s and TV, don't expect anything more than lots of innuendo. Unusual cast features Myrna Loy, Nanette Fabray, Robert Goulet, and Larry Storch in support.

Pursuit, December 12, 1972

Michael Crichton's follow-up to *The Andromeda Strain* was also his directorial debut: a still-timely thriller in which E.G. Marshall plans to set off a nerve gas at a political gathering. Ben Gazzara is out to stop him. This MOTW is based on Crichton's book *Binary*, which he wrote under the pseudonym John Lange. Crichton had wanted to direct after seeing the treatment given some of his novels by Hollywood, and persuaded ABC to let him do so by allowing them the rights to film his book.

• Crichton, of course, later wrote the book that turned into the hugely successful *Jurassic Park* franchise, and even directed several of his own movie scripts (*Coma*, *Westworld*).

Every Man Needs One, December 13, 1972
Decribed by ABC as "A swinging bachelor architect hires a spunky woman assistant against his better judgment and the situation quickly develops into a battle of the sexes." Mixing politics with comedy is a tricky brew, and when you have Ken Berry as a chauvinist pig (really!) who hires feminist Connie Stevens (really?!) to work for him, then tumbles for her, you're straining credulity … *really*. This is a lame, out-of-date Jerry Paris-directed comedy. With support from Gail Fisher (*Mannix*) and Henry Gibson (*Laugh-In*).

*** *Weekend Nun***, December 20, 1972
She's (Joanna Pettet) a naïve, novice nun! She's a parole officer! Can she be both? Will there be a crisis of conscience? Will she piss off cynical fellow social worker Vic Morrow? You bet. Saving grace: Ann Sothern as Mother Bonaventure. Believe it or not, this Paramount pilot failure was based on a true story.

Firehouse, January 2, 1973
Yet another MOTW dealing with a fish-out-of-water racial experience, in this case, what happens at a firehouse when its first African-American member (Richard Roundtree) joins up. *The Evening Standard* of Uniontown, Pennsylvania, said, "Richard Roundtree and Vince Edwards star in this highly-touted drama about racism in an all-white firefighting company, which benefits from a decent script, realistic surroundings, and good performances by the stars. An Archie Bunker-type blue-collar fireman (Edwards) leads his closely-knit company in hazing a new black recruit (Roundtree). While attempting to

break racial barriers in the dormitory atmosphere of the white firehouse, Roundtree's fireman endures continual slurs, until he finally earns the grudging respect of the company. The duel between Edwards' hard-eyed station leader and Roundtree's smoldering black man is generally effective." Smoldering? Damn right! We're talkin' 'bout *Shaft*!

The Devil's Daughter, January 9, 1973

Creepy (as she often was in her later career roles) Shelley Winters befriends waif Belinda Montgomery (in the Kim Darby role), whose mother was chummy with Winters back in the day when they worshipped Satan. If you've seen enough of these, you can guess what happens: Belinda turns out to be Satan's little girl, who discovers she is fated to couple with a demon. An obvious *Rosemary's Baby* rip-off, this flick is nonetheless fun to watch as Winters devours everything in her orbit. Holding their own are Robert Foxworth, Martha Scott, Joseph Cotten, Diane Ladd, and Abe Vigoda.

• Look for *Dark Shadows'* own Barnabas, Jonathan Frid, in a rare role as a mute servant. Frid, who was an acclaimed Shakespearean actor before landing the plum role of daytime's first vampire, has admitted that he sometimes had trouble memorizing the dozens of pages of dialogue required for each daily episode. That certainly wouldn't have been a problem on this film, since his character didn't speak!

Trouble Comes to Town, January 10, 1973

Another racial-themed drama within a week, and it wasn't even Black History Month. A Southern sheriff (Lloyd Bridges) houses a troubled African-American boy (Thomas Evans, the son of a soldier who saved the sheriff's life in Korea). Wife Sheree North is against it ("I won't have that boy in our house!"), and when someone starts stealing cars in the neighborhood, many suspect she's right to distrust the kid. In fact, the town (Colusa County in northern California substituted for the South) does split along racial lines, but the writing and acting holds up, and the movie doesn't descend into exploitative cinema as did so many feature films of the same ilk and era.

Female Artillery, January 17, 1973

Dennis Weaver has stolen money from his gang and is on the run from them. Ida Lupino, Linda Evans, Sally Anne Howes, and Nina Foch are part of a group of bawdy frontier women abandoned by their wagon train (no they're not prostitutes—Lupino and Foch? Heaven forbid!—they just refused to abandon a severely ill child). They are forced to team up to fight the gang in an abandoned cavalry fort in this proto-feminist Western. (Shouldn't Quentin Tarantino remake this film using the title and making the women prostitutes?)

Go Ask Alice, January 24, 1973

Directed by John Korty and based on a book by "Anonymous" (which was a diary of a teenager's slide into drug addiction), this cautionary tale of drug abuse and redemption took its title from the Jefferson Airplane classic about getting high, in which the listener is admonished to "Go ask Alice … when she's 10 feet tall," among other things. The Airplane song was itself a wicked riff on the adventures the young heroine had in the classic *Alice's Adventures in Wonderland*. Newcomer Jaime Smith-Jackson underplayed Alice quite nicely; *Star Trek*'s William Shatner played her confused dad; and Andy Griffith was the kindly priest who enabled Alice to get help for her addiction. This TV movie has gained an aura of prestige over the years, and rightly so; it's one of the few movies period to deal honestly with the myriad emotions, social problems and pressures that cause, and come with, addiction. Robert Carradine (*Revenge of the Nerds* and its sequels) and Mackenzie Philips—the *One Day at a Time* co-star, whose own battles with addiction are well-documented—had small roles. This quote from Alice pretty much sums up how the late 1960s and early 1970s were for many young people: "He's getting high just talking about getting high, and you're getting high off of his high, and I'm getting high off of your high. And it's one big contact high."

• Smith-Jackson's career was hot for while in the 1970s. Her film and TV credits mostly fall within a five-year period from 1973–'78, except for one TV movie and some voiceover work in the 1980s and 1990s. She did, however, appear in the classic *All the President's Men*, and one of my other favorite MOTWs, *Satan's School for Girls* (see Season Five). She is married to Canadian actor Michael Ontkean (*The Rookies, Twin Peaks*); they have two daughters.

Andy Griffith comforts Jamie Smith-Jackson in one of the first TV treatments of drug-addiction, *Go Ask Alice*. Photofest

A Cold Night's Death (a.k.a. ***The Chill Factor***), January 30, 1973

Predating John Carpenter's remake of *The Thing* by almost a decade, this tidy little horror film is similarly themed and one of the best MOTW thrillers. Basically a character study of two scientists, one older and by-the-book (Eli Wallach) and the other a younger, more maverick type (Robert Culp), as they test the effect of altitude on primates in an isolated polar research facility. But who's opening the windows? What happened to the food? Wallach tries to rationalize the mysteries as part of a high-altitude Arctic thing, but Culp thinks they may have company. And by the way ... the previous researcher at the facility has mysteriously disappeared. Is someone—or some*thing*—experimenting on the experimenters? Find this one if you can and watch it in the dead of winter with the lights out.

Snatched, January 31, 1973

If one kidnapping is suspenseful, then won't three be all the more? That's the premise behind this movie, in which three women are held for ransom by a kidnapper, but one of the husbands doesn't want to pay up. Unfortunately, the movie can't decide if it's a thriller or soap opera. With Leslie Nielsen and Sheree North, John Saxon and Barbara Parkins, and Howard Duff and Tisha Sterling as the three couples.

• The raucous 1986 Bette Midler-Danny DeVito comedy *Ruthless People* played the same situation (husband won't pay for kidnapped wife) for ironic laughs, and was a big-screen hit.

Divorce His, February 6, 1973
Divorce Hers, February 7, 1973
Elizabeth Taylor and Richard Burton teaming up in their only made-for-TV movies (made while the couple was heading for disaster in real life) is the main reason to see this routine pair of films. They were originally broadcast over two nights, and the tagline might well have been "There are two sides to every story." The first movie unveils the man's side of the split, and the second, the woman's. Taylor and Burton were much more fun to watch in real life. Instead, rent *Who's Afraid of Virginia Woolf?*, which showcases the acting couple at their best, and is uncensored.

The Great American Beauty Contest, February 13, 1973
Just in time for Valentine's Day, a look behind the scenes at a quintessentially American phenomenon: the beauty pageant. Robert Cummings, Eleanor Parker, and Louis Jourdan add weight to the proceedings, and some of the beauties include Playmate Barbi Benton and Farrah Fawcett. With *Match Game* wisecracker Brett Somers as "Miss Texas Chaperone." *Contest* fares better as a campy look back at a bruised, if not dying, American tradition. The 1975 movie *Smile* did it much better, and was *meant* to be a satire.
• The actress who played the contest winner, JoAnna Cameron, went on to play *Isis* in the short-lived 1975 kiddie super-heroine series.

The Girls of Huntington House, February 14, 1973
Social Issue Alert, I: Huntington House is a home for unwed mothers, and this tear-jerker milks their problems for all it's worth. Still, you'll never see a cast like these women together again: Oscar winners Shirley Jones (the emotionally distant English teacher who begins to get involved with her students'

problems), Mercedes McCambridge (school headmistress) and Sissy Spacek (an unwed teen); and *Dynasty*'s Pamela Sue Martin (a pouty, unwed teen), who never won an Oscar, or an Emmy for that matter, but deserved *something* for all her TV pouting and suffering. William Windom played Shirley's helpful boyfriend. This was produced by Lorimar, the folks who brought you the vastly homier *The Waltons*.

A Brand New Life, February 20, 1973

Social Issue Alert, II: Cloris Leachman (who rivaled Suzy Pleshette and Sheree North for multiple MOTW appearances) and Martin Balsam are, shall we say, of a certain age, and have remained childless, until now. What will a new baby bring to the lives of these ... *mature* adults? Leachman acquitted herself well enough to win an Emmy for her role.

And No One Could Save Her, February 21, 1973

In a plotline so good the MOTW folks recycled it (more than once!), Lee Remick stars in this paranoid thriller about a woman whose husband disappears, this time after a flight to Ireland. Janet Leigh (see *Honeymoon with a Stanger*, Season One) and Cloris Leachman (see *Dying Room Only*, Season Five) could identify with Remick.

• There are several firsts associated with this MOTW: It was Remick's first TV movie, and the first American film produced by the Robert Stigwood Organization (RSO), which would go on to produce the late-seventies blockbusters *Grease* and *Saturday Night Fever*, among others.

**The Connection*, February 27, 1973

Charles Durning (playing a crime reporter with allegiances on both sides of the law) and Ronny Cox headline this heist movie, with rare acting showcases for Howard Cosell,

Heather MacRae, Zohra Lampert, and Dennis Cole. That was not a mistake: Howard Cosell. Yup. Oh, all right, he played himself, which was probably his favorite thing in the world to do. A series would have followed the reporter's ongoing investigations.

You'll Never See Me Again, February 28, 1973

Yet another twist on the "disappearing spouse" plot device, only this time, it's a man searching for his wife. David Hartman and his bride (Jess Walton) have their first argument, during which he slaps her, she falls and bloodies her nose. She packs and leaves, saying, "You'll never see me again." Hartman, ashamed, tries to find her and apologize, but when he follows her to her parents' house, her mother (Jane Wyatt) and stepfather (Ralph Meeker) don't seem to know where she is (or even that much about her). His frantic search leads to him becoming a suspect in his wife's disappearance. Or is it murder? Joseph Campanella, Ben Gazzara, and Bo Svenson give good support.

• Walton went on to a long career in soaps, first on *Capitol*, then spending two decades on *The Young and the Restless* as Jill Abbott.

The Letters, March 6, 1973
Letters From Three Lovers, October 3, 1973

We know the U.S. Postal Service has some problems, but nothing like ones caused by a year-long delay in the delivery of the title letters to characters like Leslie Nielsen, Barbara Stanwyck, John Forsythe, Lesley Ann Warren, Dina Merrill, Jane Powell, and Ida Lupino. This pilot for an anthology-type drama series by Spelling/Goldberg productions spawned a second pilot in Season Five, seven months later. Both MOTWs featured Henry Jones as Mr. Ames, the postman. The tardy letters that cause so much trouble in the sequel are received by a young couple separated by a jail sentence; a suburban housewife having an affair; and vacationers pretending to be rich. The second pilot featured June Allyson, Ken Berry, Juliet Mills, and Martin Sheen. (Bet you never thought you'd see *those* names in the same flick!) Spelling finally got the anthology thing right in two smash hit series: *The Love Boat* (1977-'86) and *Fantasy Island* (1978-'84), both of which sprung from ABC movie pilots (though not this series).

* *The Six Million Dollar Man*, March 7, 1973

Lee Majors played an astronaut who, after a deadly crash, is retrofitted with atomic-powered body parts (some sources say "nuclear" parts); hence the birth of a new technology: bionics. It's since become part of our language: Webster's defines *bionic* as "having normal biological capability or performance enhanced by or as if by electronic or electromechanical devices." There were several sequels before the series took off, including *The Six Million Dollar Man: Wine, Women and War*, October 20, 1973; and *The Six Million Dollar Man: Solid Gold Kidnapping*, November 17, 1973. The series viewer could always tell when Majors was using his bionic legs to run: special synthesized music would start on the soundtrack and the film would be run in slow motion. The series ran from January 1974 to March 1978.

• The movies and series were based on the book *Cyborg*, by Martin Caidin; in fact, *Cyborg* was the first title for the original MOTW.

• Majors, of course, was supermodel and *Charlie's Angel* Farrah Fawcett's first husband (they married in July 1973). Fawcett appeared in four episodes of the series, as Major Kelly Wood in two episodes, and two other characters in between.

• The series birthed a spin-off called *The Bionic Woman* in a two-part pilot. Starring Lindsay Wagner in the title role (Jaime Sommers), it ran from 1976–'78, half as long as the parent show. Though the TV-movie pilot for the show debuted in March 16, 1975, it was not part of the MOTW series and was produced by Universal Television. The series did, however, air on ABC, as did the original, but only for its first season; it moved to NBC for the 1977-'78 season. Wagner and Majors each guest-starred eight times on the other's series. Wagner won the Emmy Award in 1977 for Outstanding Lead Actress in a Drama Series, and was twice nominated for a Golden Globe as Best TV Actress.

• Richard Anderson appeared as head of the Office of Scientific Intelligence (OSI) in all the TV movies and both series.

• Majors and Wagner continued playing the bionic couple after their series ended, including the made-for-TV movies *The Return of the Six Million Dollar Man and the Bionic Woman* (May 17, 1987); *Bionic Showdown*, April 30, 1989, featuring Sandra Bullock as a bionic girl in a pre-*Speed* role; and *Bionic Ever After*, November 29, 1994, in which Steve and Jaime got hitched. All three co-starred Anderson and featured Majors' son, Lee Majors II, in a supporting role as Jim Castilian.

• Another potential spin-off, *The Bionic Boy*, was filmed as a pilot and aired on November 7, 1976, featuring Majors and Vincent Van Patten as the title character. Van Patten gets bionic legs after a landslide injures him and kills his dad; he then sets out to save his dad's reputation, with a little help from Steve Austin. The ABC pilot was not picked up as a series.

• In 2001, the World Entertainment News Network reported Lee Majors blamed his role as the bionic man "for ruining his body." The then 62-year-old explained, "When I would jump into a scene, I always had to land stiff-legged and couldn't go down on my hands because I was bionic. I had to absorb it all in my knees, and all that sudden impact really killed them. The bionic man has got to go in and be rebuilt."

• Comedian Jim Carrey was briefly attached to star in an updated version of the MOTW that, no doubt, would have been long on gimmicks and comedic content. Witness this comment from Carrey: "Six million dollars doesn't get you a lot in this world these days, so you can imagine where the plot's going to go." But JimCarreyOnline reported on January 28, 2005, that the deal was off. Which made many who loved the original show breathe a sigh of relief.

• An updated *Bionic Woman*—starring British actress Michelle Ryan (*EastEnders*) as Jaime Sommers—debuted on NBC in September 2007, but never caught on with the audience. Its plot was over-complicated, its tone very dark and government-conspiracy oriented, and there was lots of bloody violence. Its chances of surviving ended when the three-month writer's strike began in early November 2007.

The Bait, March 13, 1973

Another Aaron Spelling venture, this projected pilot centered on a policewoman chosen to be the lure for a serial rapist. The *Bridgeport* (Connecticut) *Telegram* practically yawned in print at this pilot: "Another police show pilot with a slight twist— Donna Mills plays a policewoman acting as bait to catch a demented murderer. Heroine Mills, who specializes in wide-eyed looks of terror, may be protected by three detectives, but she manages to walk down dark empty streets, which creates moments of suspense." Michael Constantine (*Room 222*) and June Lockhart (*Lassie, Lost in Space*) supported. The networks didn't bite. Interestingly, just a year later prime time made room for the hit *Police Woman* and Sgt. Pepper Anderson (played by Angie Dickinson).

Class of '63, March 14, 1973

At a 10-year college reunion, Joan Hackett and Cliff Gorman are a troubled married couple heading up the list of attendees. But Gorman has more than catching up on his mind, setting a deadly trap for James Brolin, his former rival for Hackett's affections. A well-written teleplay and good acting, especially by Hackett, make this worth watching. Filmed at the University of Southern California, with scenes shot at Princeton University cut in.

Beg, Borrow, or Steal, March 20, 1973

A caper movie with a twist: The three men planning this robbery are all disabled—one is blind, one has no hands, and one is legless. Or, as a press release put it, after trying (and failing) to open a Laundromat, "Three handicapped men test their courage and abilities by plotting and executing a daring heist after they lose their jobs." With Mike (*Mannix*) Connors, Kent (*Adam-12*) McCord, and Michael (*The Mod Squad*) Cole, plus *Gilligan's Island*'s Russell Johnson and *Barney Miller*'s Detective Harris, Ron Glass, in supporting roles.

*Toma, March 21, 1973

This was pretty much your standard hard-boiled but lovable detective showcase, first in this movie and then for one year (1973-'74) as a series. When star Tony Musante quit after one year, after being denied a salary increase, producers reportedly wanted to replace him with equally swarthy (and even quirkier) Robert Blake, a la the Darrin switch on *Bewitched*. But Blake preferred to create his own character, not perform in a role created by someone else, and thus was born *Baretta* (1975–'78). Real-life Jersey cop David Toma, whose story this was, made cameo appearances in this movie and every episode of the series.

• Philip Michael Thomas played Sam Hooper in the MOTW and three episodes of the series a decade before he hit it big as Tubbs in *Miami Vice*.

• Blake went on to become a highly visible Hollywood murder suspect, accused but ultimately acquitted of shooting his wife, Bonnie.

Season Five: 1973–1974

Deliver Us From Evil, September 11, 1973

This thriller about human nature shows what transpires when a group of guys who go hiking—including George Kennedy, Bradford Dillman, Jack Weston, and Jan-Michael Vincent—happens upon a thief, who's made off with more than half a million dollars. They promptly shoot him, and begin fighting over the money. Finally, they agree to split it and go home, but nature and greed conspire to work against them. Was reality TV born from this?

• Director Boris Sagal was the father of actresses Katy, Liz, and Jean Sagal.

• The plot was reworked for the big screen in 1998 called *A Simple Plan*—three men, two of them brothers, find millions in a crashed plane that no one is looking for—directed by Sam Raimi (the *Spider-Man* big-screen franchise and the cult favorite *Evil Dead*).

She Lives!, September 12, 1973

Not a horror flick, but an early entry in the "fatal disease of the week" genre, this MOTW starred Desi Arnaz Jr. before he was derailed by drugs and personal problems, playing the father of a dying child, searching for the cure. Season Hubley, a decent actress once married to Kurt Russell, plays his wife. And Jack Soo played a rare Asian professional. If you like to cry, this is your flick. **Spoiler**: If you want to know how it ends, read the title again, slowly.

Dying Room Only, September 18, 1973

A middle-aged couple (Cloris Leachman and Dabney Coleman) makes the mistake of taking a break from driving at a desert diner late at night. Coleman goes to the men's room and never returns. Sinister Ross Martin is the diner's owner. Leachman spends the rest of the movie in jeopardy, trying to convince the police and the sheriff that she isn't imagining things. Unlike many modern suspense movies, this one actually has a "happy" ending. The MOTW used the same husband-goes-missing bit earlier in flicks starring Janet Leigh (*Honeymoon with a Stranger*) and Lee Remick (*And No One Could Save Her*), but Leachman does herself proud here, aided by Martin, Ned Beatty, and the underrated Louise Latham. Big-screen movies also found success using variations of this plot, including 1988's *Frantic*; the 1988 suspense classic *The Vanishing* and its 1993 American remake; and 1997's Kurt Russell vehicle, *Breakdown*. It's a testament to the power of Leachman's performance that her TV movie stands up to any of the big-screen efforts.

Satan's School for Girls, September 19, 1973

Tagline: A Perfect 666

A distressed young woman is driving in a car, erratically. At first, we don't know why she seems so upset. Turns out she's heading home to hang herself. Thus begins one of the best-remembered MOTWs. The girl's sister decides to get to the bottom of her sibling's suicide and enrolls at her old private school, where roomies Kate Jackson and Cheryl Stoppelmoor (later, Ladd)—that's right, two *Angels* for the price of one!— are nice but somehow ... weird. They're nothing compared to hard-ass headmistress Jo Van Fleet. But the real problem lies in the basement of the school, where you-know-who holds dominion. It's alternately creepy and silly, and occasionally both at the same time, but the acting is generally fine. Jackson is perfectly eerie, and Ladd is game, but her part is very small. Yet another Aaron Spelling cheese-fest.

• Jackson gets bonus points for playing the college dean (Van Fleet's role) in a 2000 remake that has nothing otherwise to recommend it—unless you're a Shannon Doherty fan, because she starred in it. "Is that the worst title you've ever heard in your life? It's stunning that anyone would want to remake this," Jackson told Beth Harris of the Associated Press in a March 13, 2000, interview. Harris noted that, "Despite fond memories of filming the original, Jackson so despises the movie's title that she insists on calling it *The School*. 'There's a certain amount of suspension of belief you have so you can pull it off for the audience,' Jackson said, 'but you hope you're not going to be remembered for *The School*.'" As for Spelling, when prompted about the MOTW he claimed, "I barely remember the first one. After 138 TV movies, they all kind of run together." Harris noted the original lacked the high-tech special effects of the remake, "including a fiery, chandelier-busting ending that is particularly gruesome for Jackson's character. 'Aaron is one of the masters and I love this: he puts his tongue firmly in his cheek and marches on,' Jackson said."

I love Jackson in almost anything, but *come on*, that's a classic title!

Smile When You Say "I Do", September 25, 1973
This is a rare (and sole) departure for the MOTW series: a documentary by Allen Funt, in the style of his long-running TV show, *Candid Camera*. In it, as one might deduce from the title, Funt turns the camera on scores of people, all ages and types, with the common thread that they are all filmed at wedding receptions. Essentially, it's an extended version of the series, and at 74 minutes, it fits the MOTW format (that

is, a 90-minute slot including commercials). Also described as "a comic look at marriage," the film featured such stunts as Funt convincing a couple to be married as then-popular country/novelty singer Ray Stevens ("Gitarzan," "Everything Is Beautiful," "The Streak") serenades them. If this is your thing, as they used to say, you'll enjoy the movie.

Hijack, September 26, 1973

Aaron Spelling brings you the story of two good-guy truckers offered a small fortune (well, $6,000 and a driver's license re-instatement) to take some "top secret" freight across country. David Janssen and Keenan Wynn (in an infrequent TV appearance) are the truckers.

• If the plot sounds familiar, perhaps you recall *Le Salaire de la Peur*, or *The Wages of Fear*, a taut 1953 suspenser in which Yves Montand has to haul nitroglycerine through a South American jungle. Then, the other truckers become competitive and, well, the cargo *is* an explosive…. *Hijack* is the TV-friendly version of a similar tale. Or perhaps you saw the first remake, 1977's *Sorcerer*, starring Roy Scheider.

Runaway!, September 29, 1973

In this case, what's running away is a train in the mountains, filled with passengers, facing a snowy railway. Or, as ABC put it, "An idyllic ski weekend comes to a close with a group of passengers boarding a train to return to their regular lives…. For engineer Holly Gibson (Ben Johnson), it will be his last trip before retirement." Right there you *know* something's going to go wrong. Sure enough, the brakes freeze. Passengers have to put their personal problems aside in an effort to save all aboard. Co-starring TV names Ben Murphy, Ed Nelson, Darleen Carr, Martin Milner, and "special guest star" Vera Miles. Filmed in Denver.

Isn't It Shocking?, October 2, 1973
Directed by John Badham, who went on to helm *Saturday Night Fever* and the 1979 *Dracula* (with Frank Langella), this was a departure for the typical MOTW: a horror-comedy, one of the first such hybrids. A small town with a largely, er, *mature* population becomes something less than a safe haven for seniors. The sheriff (lanky Alan Alda) is upset when the senior citizens in Mount Angel begin dropping dead in similar ways amid other weird happenings. To make matters worse, none of the victims have been robbed, and none had any notable enemies. A one-of-a-kind cast, including Louise ("Love her or hate her") Lasser as Alda's assistant/kinda love interest, Ruth Gordon as a potential victim, Lloyd Nolan, and Will Geer as a chain-smoking coroner, make this an entertaining and often funny *whatdunnit*. Filmed on a private farm in Mount Angel, Oregon, the movie is set in a bucolic *New England* village—Vermont specifically.

**The Alpha Caper (a.k.a. *Crime*) October 6, 1973
Another man wronged by his job, in this case a parole officer forced to retire, engineers a huge heist using ex-"clients" and other masterminds who are experts in various types of thievery. Distinguished mainly by the appearance of Henry Fonda, who almost never did TV. The cast for this unsold pilot was filled with former, future and current series regulars: Leonard Nimoy (*Star Trek*, *Mission: Impossible*), Elena Verdugo (*Marcus Welby, M.D.*), Vic Tayback (*Alice*), James B. Sikking (*Hill Street Blues*) and Larry Hagman (*I Dream of Jeannie*, *Dallas*).
• The proposed series, also called *Crime*, would have focused on one complicated, "foolproof" crime each week, dissecting what happened.
• Steven Bochco, one of the writers, would later work with Sikking on *Blues*.

• Producer Harve Bennett would later work with Nimoy on several *Star Trek* movies.

*Shirts/Skins, October 9, 1973

A great male cast of 1970s TV icons—including Bill Bixby, Doug McClure, McLean Stevenson, and Robert Walden— invigorates this well-remembered movie about a somewhat friendly after-work basketball competition turning less friendly, and morphing into something else. Following a rancorous game, the men change the stakes: each team will conceal a basketball downtown—in plain sight—for the other team to find. This black comedy reveals the sometimes-ugly truth behind every sports competition and exposes the lie of the cliché "It's not whether you win or lose, it's how you play the game." Rene Auberjonois and Leonard Frey are also in the game.

• This movie begat a half-hour pilot with the premise that the six guys who met for basketball each week get involved in various crazy adventures. Only Frey reprised his role.

• The movie and pilot were produced and written by Bruce Paltrow, Gwyneth's father, also known for the series *St. Elsewhere* and *The White Shadow* (all about high school basketball).

• Bixby was in between hit series (*The Courtship of Eddie's Father* and *The Incredible Hulk*) when he did this movie. Stevenson had just left the hit show *M*A*S*H*. Auberjonois would have his greatest success as the shape-shifting alien, Odo, on *Star Trek: Deep Space Nine*. Frey is best remembered for his role as the self-loathing gay man whose birthday is being celebrated in *The Boys in the Band*. Robert Walden found series success on both *Lou Grant* and Showtime's *Brothers*. McClure did a series of well-remembered campy sci-fi movies in the '70s and '80s, including *The Land that Time Forgot* and *Humanoids from the Deep*.

Don't Be Afraid of the Dark, October 10, 1973
Tagline: Now you see them … now you don't … now you die!

If you saw these creatures all over your house, you'd want your spouse to know about it, right? Kim Darby tries to convince her husband and others that she's not crazy, in *Don't Be Afraid of the Dark.* Photofest

Tiny demonic creatures are living in the Victorian house that Sally and Alex Farnham (played by Kim Darby and Jim Hutton, Timothy's dad) just moved into—and they want the wife! Why? It seems her father … but I don't want to spoil the fun. With Alex away a lot on business, oblivious Sally feels the need to redecorate and finds a locked room. Urged by the knowing and cranky handyman (William Demarest, playing to type) not to open the door to that room—"Some doors are better left unopened!"—she, of course, forces him to open it. The real horrors begin when she and her decorator (Pedro Armendáriz Jr.) tear open the bricked-up fireplace: The decorator dies soon after, falling down the stairs in an accident meant for Sally. Sally begins to see tiny, horrific creatures everywhere, but no one else does, or believes her, not even her best friend (Barbara Anderson). There follow many terrifying moments (creepy, hushed voices calling her name, a candle blown out, tiny hands locking the windows and doors). This chiller is brimming over with eerie atmosphere. And don't expect the standard Hollywood happy ending, either. Produced by Lorimar, way off *The Waltons* path.

• Felix Silla, who played one of the creatures, was better known as Cousin Itt on *The Addams Family* … a series scored by Vic Mizzy, who also did the honors for this wicked little movie.

• A remake of this movie was being planned circa 2002, but never happened. *The Hollywood Reporter* announced on July 30, 2008 that horror and fantasy writer/director Guillermo Del Toro (*Hellboy*, *The Hobbit*) and Miramax will produce a remake of *Don't Be Afraid of the Dark*. According to Gregg Goldstein, "Comic book artist-writer Troy Nixey will make his feature directorial debut with the adaptation of ABC's 1973 cult classic. Del Toro is adapting Nigel McKeand's teleplay with Matthew Robbins, his writing partner on the 1997 horror film *Mimic*." The plot will differ slightly from the MOTW: the new *Dark* will center "on a young girl, sent to live with her father and his new girlfriend, who discovers sinister creatures that live underneath the stairs. … The film is in its early stages; moviegoers can expect an upscale creature feature along the lines of Del Toro's *Pan's Labyrinth*." The new film has some big shoes to fill if Del Toro's hoping to erase memories of the original.

Double Indemnity, October 13, 1973
This is one that makes you ask, "Why bother?" Why remake a classic film that can't possibly be duplicated, let alone improved on? Oh, well … director Gus Van Sant tried it in 1998 with

Psycho, and though that remake had a talented cast, it was just so-so, until you compared it to the original, and then it was clearly inferior in every aspect. But no doubt Hollywood will keep on trying to outdo itself as long as there's the lure of a cash payoff. The cast here is good enough, but Richard Crenna, Samantha Eggar, and Lee J. Cobb can't touch Fred MacMurray, Barbara Stanwyck, or Edgar G. Robinson of the Billy Wilder-directed original.

Third Girl from the Left, October 16, 1973

From Playboy Productions came this tale of an aging chorine (Kim Novak) who questions where her life is headed. Tony Curtis co-stars, and this film is notable mainly for the two stars making their TV-movie debut. Hugh Hefner made sure then-love (and Playmate) Barbi Benton was in the cast.

• Supporting player George Furth (Zimmy) specialized in portraying fussy, swishy supporting characters who often came across as fey, if not gay. He's also an accomplished stage writer, having written plays and books for musicals, and won a 1970 Tony award for *Company*.

The Man Who Could Talk to Kids, October 17, 1973

Scott Jacoby was the seventies' go-to kid actor for sensitive, emotionally complex kids and teens. Here, he plays a disturbed teen who won't listen or talk to anyone except sympathetic counselor Peter Boyle (in a real change-of-pace role if you only know him as the gruff but lovable dad on *Everybody Loves Raymond*.) With *Willy Wonka*'s Denise Nickerson, Tyne Daly, and papa Brady himself, Robert Reed.

• Try though he might, Reed, a fine actor, could not escape the *Brady Bunch* image cultivated in five seasons (and later, countless reunion shows and specials). Still, he was already appearing in MOTWs like this one, which gave him a chance to return to the dramatic material he played in his youth, like *The Defenders* (1961-'65). Reed was nominated for a third Emmy (he never won) for his supporting role in the landmark 1977 miniseries *Roots*.

• Nickerson, best known as Violet Beauregard in *Willie Wonka & the Chocolate Factory*, appeared again with Reed in a 1974 episode of *The Brady Bunch*, "Two Petes in a Pod." (See the Foreword for more.)

Money to Burn, October 27, 1973

A cast including E.G. Marshall, Mildred Natwick, Alejandro Rey, Cleavon Little, and David Doyle enlivens this caper about a counterfeit money scheme. The casting is typical of the MOTW's patented formula: using actors who are well known to viewers from either TV (Marshall in *The Defenders*, Rey in *The Flying Nun* and Doyle in *Bridget Loves Bernie*) or the movies (Little in *Cotton Comes to Harlem*, Natwick in *Barefoot in the Park*). This was also advertised as *The ABC Suspense Movie* in some of the local TV guides the week it aired.

• "E.G. Marshall is having some second thoughts about a role he is playing in *Money to Burn*," TV reporter Leona Pappas of the *San Antonio Express* wrote on October 27, 1972. "Marshall stars as Jed Finnegan, an ingenious convict who uses the warden to smuggle out $1 million he has counterfeited while in prison. The money is to go to his wife. 'After people see this,' he said, 'and I go into a supermarket to pay, there may be a little more scrutiny when I pay the clerk!' Marshall's co-star in the film is an old friend, Mildred Natwick. 'We appeared many times together in live television, in programs like *Studio One*. This was a reunion for us.'"

• Natwick was then starring in the short-lived NBC series *The Snoop Sisters*, with Helen Hayes. She and Hayes had co-starred in the MOTW *Do Not Fold, Spindle, or Mutilate* (see Season Three).

Ordeal, October 30, 1973

Diana Muldaur, a great unsung actress of her day, plays one of her patented roles, a spiteful woman. This time, she strands her husband (Arthur Hill) in the Arizona desert and runs off with her younger lover (James Stacy). Will Hill survive to exact revenge? Perhaps experience a life-changing event that will profoundly affect the once-ruthless businessperson? Would I be asking these questions if the answers were no? Hill was starring at the time in his popular series *Owen Marshall: Counselor at Law* (1971-'74) as a good-guy attorney, so this role was like a juicy filet for him.

• Red Rock Canyon in California's Mojave Desert substituted for Arizona because, said producer William Bloom, "We searched in Arizona for weeks, but all the desert areas there were so green from heavy rainfall that we couldn't use them and we ended up 90 miles from Hollywood." ABC's press release added that, "Travel into the location site was no cinch, however. As Red Rock Canyon is a state-owned park, it is against the law for any company or individual to build roads into the area. To get to the top of the hill seen in the movie, drivers had to follow in the tracks of the preceding car—and pray a little."

• "It's a complete change of characterization for Hill," bleated ABC, "who stars weekly in the title role of *Owen Marshall, Counselor at Law*. Instead of his usual impeccably tailored suits and well-groomed appearance, he wears dirty, tattered slacks and shirt, and [sports] an ever-increasing growth of beard. In the key role of a ruthless businessman who is abandoned by his wife and her lover after he is injured in a fall, Hill is left to die on a narrow shelf with a 400-foot drop.

"When the drama opens, Hill is fat and flabby. To achieve this look, his cheeks were puffed out with sponge rubber and his clothes were three sizes too large and well-padded. As the drama progresses, smaller size slacks and shirts were worn. His beard, which had to appear to grow, was applied daily by makeup man Walter Schenck in a 40-minute, painstaking process, in which human hairs imported from China were applied individually to the actor's face. To sustain the character during his ordeal, the only food given to him by the script's writers were flowers and moths." Yum!

Guess Who's Been Sleeping in My Bed?, October 31, 1973

The ex-husband, his new wife and baby (and their dog, too, for good measure)—that's who. But when the first wife is Barbara Eden, and the hubby is Dean Jones, expect some Disney-like situation comedy, but nothing heavy about divorce or any other nasty subject. Though this was ABC Circle Films' idea of a comedy, the unlikely situation would no doubt be a tragedy for many.

Linda, November 3, 1973

Bad girl Linda (the voluptuous Stella Stevens in her prime) murders her boyfriend's wife and contrives to have her own husband charged with the crime—while the two couples are on vacation together, at the beach! Linda is loud, blowsy, sexy, pouty, and annoying, and somehow Stevens makes her fascinating despite it all. Think of this as part two of Stevens' double play (the year before she starred in a similar role in the granddaddy of all disaster films, *The Poseidon Adventure*).

The Girl Most Likely to…, November 6, 1973

When I first saw this movie, Stockard Channing mesmerized me in the title role, an ugly duckling who is humiliated by everyone because of her looks, then emerges as a beauty after a car accident necessitates plastic surgery. Does she, at this point, go out and live a wonderful life? Nooooooo…. This being a script by Joan Rivers, the heroine takes revenge by murdering her former tormentors. Looks like Joanie was exorcising some demons from her own life (and it was just a hint of things to come, as the caustic comic has admitted to tons of plastic surgery herself). What saves this from being a one-note revenge flick is the lead actress, the fabulous Channing, in one of her first starring roles. She is a sensation, and you can't take your eyes off her when she's onscreen—kinda like detective Ed Asner, who senses something suspicious going on and becomes intrigued with Channing's character despite himself. Featuring familiar TV faces Jim Backus; Joe Flynn and Carl Ballantine of *McHale's Navy*; *CHiPs'* Larry Wilcox; future *Smallville* resident Annette O'Toole; and *The Love Boat's* Gopher, Fred Grandy, in small roles. This is a prime candidate for DVD release, as the story resonates more than ever in our currently makeover-obsessed society.

• Director Lee Philips was first an actor. He made more than 50 appearances, including roles in two classic 1950s TV dramas, *Marty* and *12 Angry Men*, before switching to directing in the late 1950s. He helmed TV series as diverse as *The Donna Reed Show*, *The Waltons*, *Kung Fu*, *The Rookies*, *Space*, and *Diagnosis Murder*.

• Rivers telegrammed the following to TV-radio editor Bob Martin of the *Independent* (Long Beach, Calif.): "Until recently I thought the MOW stood for something you did to your lawn. Then my agent called me to say that they had sold my first solo comedy script to a MOW. Being new to Hollywood, I thought that was short for mogul. But when ABC-TV sent me my writer's check I suddenly got very serious about writing one of the funniest things I've ever done (pardon my immodesty), *The Girl Most Likely to….* I'm embarrassed to ask—but could you remind your readers that this is a very funny comedy? I've gotten the impression that most people think it is a drama. Thank you in advance. Now I'm going outside to Movie-of-the-Week my lawn."

• ABC called the film "a black comedy in the genre of *Kind Hearts and Coronets.*" Martin was effusive in his praise, and noted that Rivers based the plot on her own real-life humiliation "after seeing a one-time college date of hers at a party in Beverly Hills last fall. The man, now a successful doctor, was then a student at an Ivy League college and Miss Rivers was then an overly plump college girl named Joan Molinsky. She came downstairs to meet her blind date, only to hear him say, in a loud aside, 'Why didn't you tell me!' Joan, now 30 pounds lighter and a blonde instead of a brunette, wasn't recognized by the doctor, but she recognized him. 'That was the story of my college days,' she told Martin. 'I never went to a senior prom, rarely had a date at all. The night I went out with the future doctor we were home by 10 o'clock. That was romance for you.'"

• Channing told Martin she, too, had faced similar dating difficulties: "Miss Channing, who had to be turned into an ugly girl by an expert makeup artist for the first part of the film, can empathize with the character she plays. 'I had similar experiences when I was going to Radcliffe,' she says. 'I remember a Harvard boy I'd been dating who dropped me for a sexy blonde with the comment, 'Let's face it—you're no Ingrid Bergman.'" Channing has become one of the most acclaimed actors of her generation.

Death Race (a.k.a. **State of Division**), November 10, 1973
Fighter pilots Del Culpepper (Doug McClure) and Arnold McMillan (Roy Thinnes) are on a mission to destroy a German

mine field during the British 8th Army's victorious advance after the battle of El Alamein. McMillan is shot down, and Culpepper's P-40 aircraft is damaged in a rescue bid; it can't fly, but it can still taxi on the ground. That's good enough for Nazi general Lloyd Bridges, bent on their destruction—with the help of Eric Braeden, in one of his pre-*Young and the Restless* roles—who pursues the two Yanks relentlessly through the North African desert.

• The P-40, with a toothy shark's mouth painted on its nose, was one of the most recognizable fighters of World War II.

• Harve Bennett produced. He was the producer and writer of *Star Trek II, III, IV*, and *V*, plus the executive producer of *The Six Million Dollar Man* series (see Season Four).

Trapped, November 14, 1973
Or *Cujo* times six. James Brolin offers a solid performance as a regular guy, mugged and left unconscious in a department store, who discovers a half-dozen vicious Dobermans guarding the store when he tries to leave.

The Affair, November 15, 1973
Sappy vanity production produced by Aaron Spelling and starring real-life couple Natalie Wood and Robert Wagner. Lawyer (Wagner) meets disabled songwriter (Wood); he teaches her how to love. Cue the violins.

• Wood and Wagner were hoping the second time was the charm; they'd remarried in 1972 after 10 years apart. They remained together until her tragic drowning death in 1981.

Scream, Pretty Peggy, November 24, 1973
There are probably several reasons why this movie is so well-remembered: *That Girl's* boyfriend, Ted Bessell, had recently finished his long run on that sitcom, and was a well-known

and liked TV face; movie queen Bette Davis was making a rare appearance as his mother; and the plot was a riff on the mother-love theme from the classic horror film *Psycho*: young man shelters his older mother and mentally disturbed sister in a spooky house. Sian Barbara Allen plays a college student (the Peggy of the title) hired, as were other women before her, to take care of Ted's mom and sis while he sculpts. Peggy does scream a lot, especially after finding Bessell's crazy sis locked away in a secret room. Just missing the "classic suspense/horror movie" category, this film ends up a camp classic, not quite awful, not great, but worth watching due to the stars. As the *Charleston* (West Virginia) *Gazette* put it, "This melodrama strains a bit to create a few scares, but fans of Bette Davis' affinity for horror-movie roles will enjoy watching her overact tonight."

Outrage, November 28, 1973

The plot of 1974's *Death Wish* was given a dry run here, and according to the reviews—one paper called the hero's revenge "an astonishing depiction of savagery"—things get as nasty as that classic Charles Bronson film. Robert Culp takes on a gang of kids whose pranks against their upper-crust neighbors become increasingly more aggressive and ugly. Based on a real-life incident. Mark Lenard (Spock's dad on *Star Trek*) supports.

A Summer Without Boys, December 4, 1973

Summer of '42, MOTW-style: A soon-to-be-single mom (Barbara Bain) finds herself up against her daughter (Kay Lenz), vying for the affections of Michael Moriarty during World War II, when most of the men and boys were overseas protecting our country. Bain and Moriarty? I can see mom and daughter fighting over, say, Dack Rambo, but Moriarty's eccentric acting style was more suited to heavier fare—and I never saw him as a romantic lead. With *Mary Hartman*'s slutty sister, the late, wonderful Debralee Scott, playing Lenz's slutty friend.

Bloodsport, December 5, 1973

Teen Gary Busey is split between winning and doing the right thing in this football flick with a mean streak. Larry Hagman plays the "winning is everything" coach. Ben Johnson plays Busey's factory-worker dad, who wants a better life for him, but believes the only way that will happen is with a football scholarship. Jay Sharbutt, writing in the *Greeley* (Colorado) *Tribune*, said this film was the real deal: "It's an intelligent look at growing up in a small town, and is as understated and low-key as *The Last Picture Show*, which earned Johnson an Oscar a few years back."

• Busey was a real-life gridiron star at Coffeyville (Kansas) Community College.

Maneater, December 8, 1973

Ben Gazzara and MOTW staple Sheree North fight starving tigers on what they thought would be a fun camping trip. An "eccentric" (ABC's word) animal trainer (Richard Basehart), whose love for his hungry man-eaters exceeds his love for his fellow humans, has deliberately disabled their vehicle. This was the directorial debut of Vince Edwards, MOTW star and the former *Ben Casey*.

The Cat Creature, December 11, 1973

This was written by horror great Robert Bloch—known for *Psycho*, *Straight-Jacket*, *The House That Dripped Blood*, and many *Thriller*, *Alfred Hitchcock Presents* and *Star Trek*

Gale Sondergaard gets her claws out in her occult shop—you better believe she knows what's bothering the troubled Meredith Baxter in *The Cat Creature*. **Photofest**

scripts—from a story by Bloch and prolific TV producer Douglas S. Cramer. An estate appraiser arrives to inventory a recently deceased's possessions. Among other items, he discovers a mummy, topped with the head of the Egyptian cat goddess Bast, wearing a large amulet around its neck. Soon after he leaves, a thief steals the amulet, beginning a chain of events leading to multiple murders (the victims are all scratched and clawed, as if killed by a cat) and the possible reincarnation of Bast herself.

This MOTW toplined Meredith Baxter (soon to add then-spouse David Birney's name to her own) as a mysterious woman who may have a connection to the murders, and David Hedison, as an archeology professor called in by lead detective Lt. Marco (Stuart Whitman) to help out. Noteworthy for featuring top character actors who specialized in horror/thriller films, like John Carradine, Gale Sondergaard, and Keye Luke (*Gremlins*).

• Hedison was signed to a contract with 20th Century Fox in the late 1950s. His second film there, 1958's classic horror film, *The Fly*, would bring him lasting fame. More movies—among them 1960's *The Lost World* and 1965's *The Greatest Story Ever Told*—and a hit TV series, *Voyage to the Bottom of the Sea* (1964-'68) followed, plus many other film and TV roles. The actor recalled his experience filming *The Cat Creature* especially for this book; his comments follow:

"In the early seventies, over dinner at his house, Doug Cramer asked me if I would be interested in appearing in a 90-minute project he was producing for ABC, called *The Cat Creature*. He sent me the script the next morning and I agreed to join the cast—Meredith Baxter and Stuart Whitman, and, I later found out, Gale Sondergaard, whose wonderful work I remembered from so many films, particularly the Warner Bros. production of Somerset Maugham's *The Letter*, with Bette Davis.

"All in all, it was a very happy experience. Meredith was a joy to work with, and a fine human being. Stuart Whitman and I talked and laughed a lot about our early contract days at 20th Century Fox in the late 1950s and 1960s. And, of course, Gale was a lovely woman and shared so many wonderful memories with me about her early films. And I should add that all the felines behaved beautifully—even in one of the more violent scenes with me at the end of the film. I managed to escape without a scratch.

"One other memory was of the first screening of the film before it aired. There was a small invited audience at a screening room on the lot. My wife, Bridget, had not read the script or seen any of the shooting, and at one point when the Cat Creature suddenly jumps out to attack, she got such a fright she let out a scream—much to the delight of the producers and director."

• Baxter's character, Rena, was a tribute to the character played by Simone Simon, Irena, in producer Val Lewton's 1942 classic *Cat People*. Producer Cramer's initial intention was to honor the classic Hollywood horror films. In another homage, Kent Smith, who played one of the leads in Lewton's film, played the small role of the estate appraiser.

• Director Curtis Harrington also helmed the MOTW *How Awful About Allan*, not to mention dozens of TV shows (*Dynasty*, *Hotel* and *The New Twilight Zone*) and films, including two of my favorite gothic horror/Shelley Winters showcases: *Who Slew Auntie Roo?* and *What's the Matter with Helen?* When Harrington asked questions, you were never sure if you wanted the answers!

• According to the Unofficial Robert Bloch Web site, the script was originally planned to star Diahann Carroll; when she left the project, ABC wanted to cast Patty Duke, but eventually chose Baxter.

• The part of occult store proprietor Hester Black, played to sinister perfection by Oscar-winner Sondergaard, was originally written as a man.

Message to My Daughter, December 12, 1973
One of the first television movies to deal with abortion, this features a somewhat clichéd plot device—dead mom (Bonnie Bedelia) talks to her daughter (Kitty Winn) through tapes she left behind—but it was daring subject matter at the time. With Martin Sheen. Bedelia is seen in flashbacks, and her acting, and Winn's as her confused kid, raise this a notch above the traditional four-hankie picture.

• Winn would have her biggest movie hit this same year, as Ellen Burstyn's loyal secretary in *The Exorcist*.

What Are Best Friends For?, December 18, 1973

Apparently, they're good at finding mates for divorced men who have come to stay with them. Ted Bessell, Barbara Feldon, Larry Hagman, Lee Grant, and Nina Foch are all involved in the frothy fun.

***Pioneer Woman**, December 19, 1973

Joanna Pettet and her family try to set up house in pioneer-era Wyoming, but when her husband is killed, she has to choose between staying and fighting for a life on the prairie, or slinking back East. David Janssen, Helen Hunt (in her first role; she was 10 years old) and William Shatner co-star. This unsold pilot was produced by Filmways and directed by MOTW regular Buzz Kulik (*Brian's Song, Bad Ronald*).

• Shatner, best-known as the scenery-chewing Captain Kirk in the *Star Trek* franchise, made *Star Trek: The Animated Series* the same year as this MOTW. The Canadian actor has actually had one of TV's most durable careers. Among the highlights: playing *T.J. Hooker* (1982-'86) and earning two Emmys starring as Denny Crane on *Boston Legal* (2004-present).

The Death Squad, January 8, 1974

This MOTW came across as a tamer version of Clint Eastwood's 1973 *Magnum Force*, in which a detective goes undercover to smoke out a group of renegade cops (here led by *B.J. and the Bear*'s Sheriff Lobo himself, Claude Akins). Robert Forster takes the Eastwood role, and Mama Michelle Phillips is his main squeeze. Spelling-Goldberg strikes again.

Shootout in a One Dog Town, January 9, 1974

Hanna-Barbera produced this Western comedy, in which a bank teller (Richard Crenna) tries to prevent nasty robbers—aren't they always extra-nasty in these Westerns?—from taking the $200,000 he needs to deposit in his bank. Stefanie Powers co-stars, and Jack Elam (he of the skewed eye) is in fine form as the town's bartender *and* sheriff.

Mrs. Sundance, January 15, 1974

Most notable for being the second time Elizabeth Montgomery made a conscious effort to split from her *Bewitched* persona (see *The Victim* in Season Four), our Liz takes over the role created by Katharine Ross and shows what might have happened to Etta Place after Butch and Sundance were interred at Boot Hill following the classic 1969 film *Butch Cassidy and the Sundance Kid*. Not historically accurate, the MOTW survives on Montgomery's captivating persona. Co-starring Robert Foxworth, who met Montgomery on this film and became her lover and eventually her husband.

• Foxworth is shown nude, from behind, in the European theatrical version of this Western. It was common practice to shoot some additional mild nudity for the overseas market. That scene was eventually shown on American TV, illustrating how less restrictive the medium has become since the 1970s.
• In one of those only-in-Hollywood loops, Ross reclaimed the role of Etta in a second TV-movie sequel, 1976's *Wanted: The Sundance Woman* (which was *not* a MOTW).

Scream of the Wolf, January 16, 1974

Director Dan Curtis, the man behind *Dark Shadows*, and fantasy/horror writer Richard Matheson, return to familiar territory but produce only a standard monster-on-the-loose tale, coupled with a *Most Dangerous Game* plot. Starring Clint Walker and Peter Graves, with seventies icon Jo Ann Pflug (*M*A*S*H*'s Lt. Dish) adding the sex appeal … if she's your idea of a Dish.

• When is a wolf not a wolf? When it's a large German Shepherd. An article in the *Robesonian* (Lumberton, N.C.) on January 13, 1973, noted, "Hollywood wolves [the four-legged kind] aren't what they used to be.… Producer-director Dan Curtis, in looking for a large wolf to play in *Scream of the Wolf* … couldn't find one. Property master Ted Berkeley scoured the animal rental spots around Hollywood and came up with one wolf." But the wolf was too small. "I was looking for a large timber wolf type," Curtis said. "The wolf that came into the office was the size of an average dog. I needed an animal … whose size and strength boggles everyone in the story." The solution arrived when Berkeley found animal trainer Cindy James, who produced a German Shepherd that she'd spray-painted "a wolfish gray-brown." It's a good thing, too, since James noted, "Wolves are very difficult to train, almost impossible.… You can make a movie dog act mad or vicious and when the scene is over, the dog stops acting. Not so the wolf. Once he's mad, he stays mad." I'm sure the actors involved were most appreciative.

Skyway to Death, January 19, 1974

Stefanie Powers and other familiar TV faces—Ross Martin, Bobby Sherman, Tige Andrews, Nancy Malone, John Astin, and Joseph Campanella—are trapped in this movie … um, in a broken, sabotaged skyway tram, 8,500 feet up. Best thing about this MOTW: its wonderfully horrible title. Filmed on location at the Palm Springs, California, aerial tramway.

• Sherman, a former teen idol with four gold records to his credit and one series (*Here Come the Brides*), here stretched his limited chops to play the conductor/guide of the tram. Well, at least he was still cute.

Get Christie Love! starring the foxy Teresa Graves was one of many MOTW pilots that went to series. Christie was so sweet, she added the word "Sugar" to everything, even when tagging the bad guys: "You're under arrest, Sugar!" Photofest

* ***Get Christie Love!***, January 22, 1974
Tagline: She's one bad mamma jamma! This was the pilot for the short-lived (one season) but well-remembered series starring sassy Teresa Graves (of *Laugh-In* fame) as a butt-kicking cop. *Christie* was an attempt (and not an awful one) to bring blaxploitation to television. From a promo: "The cop with soul! When you need a cop that's no lady, you need Christie Love." With the catchphrase "Watch out, Sugar!" and a strategy of making herself appear helpless, thus throwing off the bad guys so she could kick ass, Christie was a lovable and, unfortunately, rare empowered ethnic woman on mid-1970s TV. That's a shame, because Graves' ebullient personality and hip, positive portrayal remains one of the better portraits of a professional black woman on television. *Get Christie Love!* followed the Wednesday MOTW at 10:00 p.m. for the 1974-'75 season.

• The episode that aired February 5, 1975, featured six of Graves' *Laugh-In* co-stars: Johnny Brown, Judy Carne, Henry Gibson, Arte Johnson, Gary Owens, and Jo Anne Worley.

• Graves guest-starred on one of TV's most memorable flops: a one-night *Laugh-In* rip-off called *Turn On* that was cancelled 10 minutes into the first show.

• Graves gave up her career after *Christie Love* to became a Jehovah's Witness. She died in the winter of 2002, the result of a faulty heater that caused a fatal fire.

Pray for the Wildcats, January 23, 1974

TV stars have done all kinds of things to try and break out of long-running, typecasting roles. Here Andy Griffith, caught in the hell between Mayberry and *Matlock* (which included 1971's *The New Andy Griffith Show*, an unsuccessful attempt to recapture the homespun charm of the original) exercised his acting chops as a bad, bad man—who runs a hugely successful company, of course. Trying out a new ad agency, he insists those working on his account visit the proposed site for a commercial, Baja California, by dirt bike. Along the way, there's a murder (not to mention a pre-*Indecent Proposal*-type offer by Griffith, to the tune of $20!) and so much more. William Shatner, Marjoe Gortner and *The Brady Bunch*'s Robert Reed are the unfortunates along for the ride. Angie Dickinson is Reed's wife, agonizing over her affair with Shatner. Equal opportunity offensiveness here: the men and the women (including *Jaws*' Lorraine Gary) are *all* stupid. Campy, sadistic fun.

Heatwave, January 26, 1974

Ben Murphy and Bonnie Bedelia play a brokerage clerk and his pregnant wife in this tale of an unusual—what else?—heat wave scorching a small town and its residents. Can they teach the other scared (and charred) residents how to survive? I'd bet my air conditioner on a "yes" if I were you. (By the way, the title is grammatically incorrect; heat wave is two words.)

The Girl Who Came Gift-Wrapped, January 29, 1974

These were the halcyon days of TV movies, when Karen Valentine (as the perky title character) got top billing over newbie Farrah Fawcett. Come to think of it, Valentine might *still* get top billing…. Here Valentine plays a small-town cutie hired by the friends of wealthy Richard Long as a birthday gift (these were also the pre-PC days). For a time—the late sixties through the seventies—Valentine was many a man's idea of the perfect gal pal. Stripping down to a bikini while singing "Happy Birthday" to Long in this cute comedy didn't hurt, either. In fact, it's a touchstone scene for many teenage boys who grew up in that era.

• Co-star Long, best known for his roles in *The Big Valley* (he played Lee Majors' brother), and as Professor Harold Everett on *Nanny and the Professor*, was an underrated actor who died at age 47 of a heart ailment the year this MOTW was filmed.

Killdozer, February 2, 1974

Based on a short novella written by horror veteran Theodore Sturgeon and published in *Astounding Science Fiction*, November 1944. Sturgeon also wrote the screenplay. This is the movie that should have convinced Stephen King not to direct his own short story, 1986's *Maximum Overdrive*, featuring huge trucks and other machines that inexplicably become man-hunting monsters. *Killdozer*'s plot takes us to an airstrip construction site on an island in the Pacific circa World War II (it was actually filmed in California). An ancient, angry and evil (Duh!) alien entity is brought to earth via a meteor. What does it do? Inhabit the construction equipment to kill the men working on building an airstrip. If I were ancient evil, I'm not sure that's the direction I'd take, but, who can really say in these matters? In any case, its retro-cool title, and the intense portrayal of mass destruction have endeared this movie to kids and *Junkyard Wars* addicts alike. In fact, it's many fans' favorite "machine inhabited by evil presence" flick. As *SCTV*'s Big Jim and Billy Sol might have said, "It blowed up *real* good."

• At the Web site www.jumptheshark.com, "jumping the shark" is "a defining moment when you know your favorite television show has reached its peak. The instant that you know from now on … it's all downhill." The *ABC Movie of the Week* has, as of this writing, five votes for a specific movie in the series being its "jump the shark" moment. The movie cited is … *Killdozer*.

• Regardless, many fans hold this film in high esteem, whether for its cheese factor or simply as enjoyably silly. These include Dave Coleman at www.bijouflix.com, who perceptively wrote, regarding *Killdozer*'s release on video, "Don't go into this one expecting great literature. Rather, it's great 'bulldozer comes to life' cinema, which should give you an idea of where to begin excavation on this rarity in terms of quality." In fact, in its wanton destruction of men, huts, and storage facilities, its "mechanical indifference … recalls the *Terminator*," Coleman concludes.

• The cast includes Carl Betz, way out of *Donna Reed* territory, and nominal (troubled alcoholic) hero Clint Walker, who huddle together at one point, trying to decide what to do with the animated machine. Betz notes, seriously, "Too heavy to hang. Won't fit in a gas chamber." Also in the cast was a young Robert Urich in his first movie role, as a Killdozer victim, coming off the flop series *Bob & Carol &Ted & Alice*.

• *Killdozer* was reprinted many times before and after the movie in various science fiction collections, and was adapted to comic book form after this MOTW in April 1974's *World's Unknown* #6 (by Gerry Conway and Dick Ayers). The comic referred to the title menace as "The thing called … KILLDOZER" and also noted on the cover, "As seen on TV!"

• Killdozer was also the name of a garage band that played noise rock, an alternative outgrowth of punk that featured atonal and industrial sounds; it released nine albums between 1983 and 1997.

Can Ellen Be Saved?, February 5, 1974

Leslie Nielsen's daughter joins a cult in search of fulfillment, a popular thing to do in the early 1970s, especially when the cult leader is the charismatic and cute Michael Parks. But Parks wants only to accumulate wealth for himself. Ellen becomes "Ruth," and her dad sends the equally cute John Saxon to rescue her and re-program her. At least one critic, Bob Foster of the *San Mateo* (California) *Times*, thought the ending needed a fix: "The methods used to 'un-program' the girl are questionable. One never knows whether she leaves to become a real Christian or is left as an agnostic, as she returns to her normal life. That question may bother a lot of viewers. It did us."

Cry Panic!, February 6, 1974

Returning to the suspense genre and delivering a hit, this MOTW finds a businessman (John Forsythe) driving from Los Angeles to San Francisco hitting a man and killing him. Unfotunately (for him), Forsythe is a good Samaritan who tries to do the right thing, but things go downhill once the police arrive and there's no body to be found. The local townspeople (including mysterious, beautiful Anne Francis and sheriff Earl Holliman) are hiding a deadly secret about the victim. Watch for a scary scene in which Forsythe discovers something in a meat locker.

• Written by Jack B. Sowards, who also wrote perhaps the best *Star Trek* movie of them all: *Star Trek II, The Wrath of Khan*.

The Elevator, February 9, 1974

Okay, we tried it in a tram (see *Skyway to Death*, January 19), let's try it in an elevator: A group of Hollywood stock characters (played by Roddy McDowall, James Farentino, Teresa Wright, Myrna Loy, Craig Stevens, and Carol Lynley), one of them "a berserk armed robber" according to ABC's press release, are trapped in a broken elevator "that could plunge 30 floors to the ground at any moment. The thief's claustrophobia and the panic of the passengers" add to the, er, fun.

• McDowall and Lynley were featured two years earlier in the disaster flick *The Poseidon Adventure*.

I Love You...Goodbye, February 12, 1974

Hope Lange plays a wife and mother beginning to question the validity of her life; she walks out on it all in a bid to find her true desires. Earl Holliman, as her puzzled husband, shows his range, going from menacing sheriff to sensitive hubby in six days (see February 6).

• According to an AP wire story on January 2, 1974, Lange had recently walked on *The New Dick Van Dyke Show*, in which she played Van Dyke's wife. Her comment to the press that, "All I ever do [on the series] is pour coffee" was what inspired Deanne Barkley (described by the AP as "the vice president in charge of the *ABC Movie of the Week*") to cast Lange in *this* MOTW. Lange's character "just gets fed up. She's a woman who got married very early and got so involved playing wife and mother that she never had time to find out who she was or what she wanted."

• Lange herself was fed up that CBS refused to air a "tastefully done" *Van Dyke Show* episode in which the couple's daughter walks in on them during the act of making love. "They won't even air the best show we did all season. To hell with it," Lange told the AP. "That's not the reason I'm leaving, but it irks me very much."

The Morning After, February 13, 1974

This is a rare message movie that doesn't fudge its ending. Dick Van Dyke loses his job and family as he descends into alcoholism. Comedian Van Dyke, nominated for an Emmy, pulled out all the stops and proved a capable dramatic actor in this well-remembered movie.

• Van Dyke publicly came out as an alcoholic two years before this MOTW, entering a treatment facility during a creatively unsuccessful three-year run on TV in *The New Dick Van Dyke Show* (1971–'74; see above). He subsequently overcame the disease and actively got involved in helping others with the same problem.

Live Again, Die Again, February 16, 1974

Donna Mills has been cryogenically frozen for 34 years; when she awakens, she finds things aren't quite perfect in her brave new world: her husband (Walter Pidgeon) is much older, naturally, and so are her kids (Vera Miles and *M*A*S*H*'s Mike Farrell). What starts as sci-fi turns into a gothic horror tale, with a rare TV performance by the wonderful Geraldine Page as their addled housekeeper. The Aniston, Alabama, *Star* noted, "A climactic sequence is marvelous: a large portion of the story is told without dialogue in a beautifully handled montage with split screen, super-impositions, and slow motion." It was directed by TV veteran Richard A. Colla (*Battlestar Galactica, Gunsmoke, Ironside, Murder, She Wrote* and many others).

Hitchhike!, February 23, 1974
A trip from Los Angeles to San Francisco takes a turn for the worse when the woman driving (Cloris Leachman, again putting her stamp on a role she perfected, the woman/wife in jeopardy) picks up a murderous hitchhiker (Michael Brandon). In this case, Leachman tries the "let's be friends" approach to throw the killer off guard.

Killer Bees, February 26, 1974
Gloria Swanson becomes Queen of the B's (literally!) as a beekeeper with a closer relationship to her insects than is normal. Edward Albert as her grandson and girlfriend Kate Jackson complicate matters. Albert and Jackson were a real-life couple for a time.

Unwed Father, February 27, 1974
Joseph Bottoms plays an adopted kid who refuses to allow his new son to be put up for adoption, resulting in a series of custody battles. Bottoms is surrounded by good veteran actors like Kim Hunter and Beverly Garland; newcomers Kay Lenz and Willie Aames also appear. As in the movie, the actors felt differently about what they'd do if the situation arose in their real lives. "I don't know," Bottoms told the Danville, Virginia *Register and Bee*. "It's something I can't answer with any degree of positiveness [sic] because there are too many things to consider, too many variables. All I can say is that I'm grateful not having to decide such a vital question in my own life." Lenz, on the other hand, "didn't hesitate when asked what she would do if faced with a problem of such urgency. 'I'd keep the baby,' she said firmly. 'I can't understand how any mother could do otherwise. No matter what the circumstance, I couldn't—I wouldn't—give my baby away to strangers.'" The

MOTW hedges its bets by leaving it open as to who is morally right and wrong.

Houston, We've Got a Problem, March 2, 1974

Fact-based tale (with fiction thrown in) of NASA's 1970 attempt to get Apollo 13 back to Earth after it suffers an explosion in space. Robert Culp, Gary Collins, and Sandra Dee star. Filmed on location in Houston.

• The title of this MOTW was also used for a 1994 documentary short. A slight revision of this title ("Houston, we have a problem") became the tagline for Tom Hanks' hit big-screen version of the same incident, 1995's *Apollo 13*.

The Stranger Who Looks Like Me, March 6, 1974

Meredith Baxter is an adopted kid searching for her real parents; her real-life mom, Whitney Blake, portrays her biological mom. Director Larry Peerce (son of opera tenor Jan Peerce) used improvisation in several of the scenes, including one in which a group of adopted children demand the right to know their true parents. He told the *Cedar Rapids* (Iowa) *Gazette*, "Everybody knew what their attitudes would be and who they were. I wanted to see what would happen in a real situation without words being put in their mouths. The realities that occurred in the scene couldn't have been written in a script."

• Peerce was at home on TV or in the movies. His best-known film was 1969's *Goodbye, Columbus*. He also worked on the campy 1966 *Batman* series.

• Blake was best known for her four-year stint as the mother on the sitcom *Hazel* (1961-'65). She also created and wrote for the long-running sitcom *One Day at a Time* (1975-'84).

* ***Wonder Woman***, March 12, 1974

Starring Cathy Lee Crosby and Ricardo Montalban as the evil Abner Smith, this MOTW was ridiculed due to the fact that Wonder Woman doesn't have superpowers and does not wear her traditional va-va-voom red,white, and blue costume. Keep in mind that's because D.C. Comics at the time had stripped its heroine of her powers and her classic uniform. They would be restored within a year, and by then TV had the right formula: *The New Original Wonder Woman* (November 7, 1975), which starred the voluptuous and athletic Lynda Carter, who became a household name starring in the series. The original Crosby version did have its charms, including Montalban and an old-fashioned, serial-type cliff-hanger ending before each commercial break. The second movie aired on ABC but was not a MOTW. It featured Cloris Leachman as Queen Hippolyta and Fannie Flagg as an Amazon doctor, not to mention Red Buttons and Stella Stevens as "Marcia." The 1976 series—*Wonder Woman*, a.k.a. *The New Adventures of Wonder Woman*— ran for three years, and also featured Lyle Waggoner as the stoic Major Steve Trevor (and then, Steve Trevor Jr.), while *The Addams Family*'s Carolyn Jones took over as Hippolyta for three episodes.

• Flagg was better known as a TV game-show panelist who was quick with a quip (on *The Match Game* from 1974–'82) and later as a best-selling author (*Fried Green Tomatoes*).

• Carter had auditioned for the original MOTW but had to wait another year before her turn at bat.

• For years, the major studios have been trying to get a *Wonder Woman* feature film into production, but no one has come up with a script or lead actress to top the classic nostalgia of this series and Carter's portrayal.

* ***The Hanged Man***, March 13, 1974

This Western offers the following strained plot, according to its press release: "A former gunslinger is unjustly hanged and pronounced dead, yet returns to life hours later as a mystical and mysterious avenger fighting for justice in the Old West." Translation: He can read minds. Starring Steve Forrest, with Dean Jagger and Will Geer. Wonder if Forrest could foretell this pilot would not be picked up.

* ***The Gun and the Pulpit***, April 3, 1974

Marjoe Gortner, a "lightning-fast" gunslinger, trades clothes with a dead preacher in order to escape hanging for a crime he didn't commit. Disguised as the Reverend Frank Fleming, he rides into a town at the mercy of a crooked boss, and shames the townspeople into regaining their self-respect. Whew. Oh, and he falls for ripe teenager Pamela Sue Martin. That might be a problem for a preacher-man. With Estelle Parsons and Slim Pickens, this Western was filmed in Old Tucson, Arizona and was an unsold pilot from Danny Thomas productions.

* ***Melvin Purvis, G-Man*** (a.k.a. ***The Legend of Machine Gun Kelly***), Tuesday, April 9, 1974

Director Dan Curtis busts another genre, the gangster film, to solid but fairly typical results. Dale Robertson stars as the flamboyant 1930s Midwest FBI bureau chief who tracks down notorious killer Machine Gun Kelly. Released theatrically in Europe in February 1975. With Harris Yulin as George 'Machine Gun' Kelly; *Bewitched*'s Dick Sargent as Thatcher Covington; David Canary (*Bonanza*, *All My Children*) as Eugene 'Gene' T. Farber; Curtis fave John Karlen as Anthony 'Tony' Redecci; and Steve Kanaly (*Dallas*) as Sam Cowley.

• Of the film's location shoot, Curtis noted at the time, "Our story is that of Purvis and his relentless hunt for Kelly and his gang. Most of the action takes place in Mississippi, and the area around Nicolaus, California, is a carbon copy." Nicolaus was dotted with still-used architecture from the 1920s and 1930s, flat farmland, wooded areas, and the Sacramento River, which doubled for the Mississippi.

• Writer William Nolan noted that Purvis founded the Melvin Purvis Junior G-Men Club when he left the FBI. "Millions of us belonged to it," Nolan recalled. "We identified with a hero."

Murder or Mercy, April 10, 1974

A lawyer (Bradford Dillman as Sam Champion … obvious name, eh?) enlists his retired dad (Denver Pyle) to defend a distinguished doctor (the always excellent Melvyn Douglas) accused of putting his sick wife (Mildred Dunnock) out of her misery. A rare film, TV or otherwise, that tackles the thorny issue of mercy killing, this Quinn Martin pilot didn't sell.

The Last Angry Man, April 16, 1974

In this remake of the 1959 classic, Pat Hingle takes on the role of a Brooklyn doctor working in the slums; Paul Muni got an Oscar nomination for the original. Paul Jabara, Oscar winner for best song in 1979 ("Last Dance") and an original cast member of Broadway's *Hair*, is the best-known actor in the supporting cast. Screen Gems' instincts were off—this projected series never sold.

* *Nakia*, April 17, 1974

White (but dark and handsome) Robert Forster is Nakia, a Native American deputy sheriff in the Southwest who survives a beating and treks across the desert to deal with his tribe's dispute over a historic mission that developers want to raze. *Nakia* became a 14-episode TV series that aired from

September through December 1974, starring Forster, Arthur Kennedy (also in the MOTW), and Gloria DeHaven.

The Chadwick Family, April 17, 1974

Part of a special MOTW double feature, this family soap opera and rejected pilot starred Fred MacMurray (in his television movie debut) as a small-town newspaper publisher dealing with various emotional crises involving his son, three daughters, and their spouses/mates, one of whom is Asian (Frank Michael Liu). Among the other actors, one gets the unusually wordy credit of "special guest star Barry Bostwick as Duffy McTaggert." Bostwick had yet to star in his best-known role (Brad Majors in 1975's cult hit *The Rocky Horror Picture Show*), so it remains a question mark as to why he got the unique credit.

* *Planet Earth*, April 23, 1974

Starring John Saxon and Diana Muldaur, and featuring Majel Barrett, this was an unusual sci-fi flop for *Star Trek*'s creator Gene Roddenberry, done after Kirk, Spock and crew finished their first TV run, but before the *Enterprise*'s first big-screen effort. Directed by Marc Daniels, the first *I Love Lucy* director; he also directed many of the original *Star Trek* episodes. In the 22nd century, 180 years in the future, life on Earth has tumbled backward after a nuclear war, and people belong to tribes in a feudal society. Saxon's character awakens from a long suspended animation and becomes part of a group called Pax (peace), whose members are Earth's surviving doctors, artist, scientists, and so on. They're trying to rebuild society; Muldaur plays the head of an Amazon-like group who wants a female-controlled society.

• *Planet Earth* began life as a CBS TV movie called *Genesis II*, written by Roddenberry, which aired in 1973 and was not picked up as a series. It starred Alex Cord as a scientist who wakes up in the 22nd century to find a war going on between the Pax proponents and mutants called Tyranians. Mariette Hartley was one of the latter, and Ted Cassidy, Percy Rodrigues, and Majel Barrett were featured. CBS decided to go to series with *Planet of the Apes* instead. According to the Associated Press, "Roddenberry took it to ABC, which liked its action-adventure potential and agreed to a pilot with a new cast," i.e., *Planet Earth*. (*Star Trek* itself was initially rejected in 1963 by CBS in favor of the cheesy *Lost in Space*.)

• Barrett, a semi-regular on the original *Star Trek* as Nurse Christine Chapel, was by this time married to Roddenberry. Her *Trek* character became a doctor and was featured in several of the *Trek* movies. She was also the voice of the *Enterprise* computer for most of the franchise's incarnations on TV and in the movies.

• Roddenberry told the AP on April 21, 1974 that, "People, not gadgets, are the mainstay of science fiction." He added, regarding the premise of *Planet Earth*, "I believe in mankind. We're extraordinary creature[s]. Our destiny is not dependent upon the materiality of this civilization. There can be few catastrophes larger than the loss of the Roman Empire. We lost that, but we rebuilt again and made it better."

The Story of Pretty Boy Floyd, May 7, 1974

Young Martin Sheen as the title character (born Charley Arthur Floyd) is desperate to escape the bleak poverty of his Oklahoma farm, but when he leaves his close-knit family, gosh darn it, he ends up becoming a criminal and one of the most notorious bank robbers of the Depression era. With the invaluable Kim Darby and a "special guest appearance" by Grandma Walton herself, Ellen Corby, as Ma Floyd.

Season Six: 1974–1975

Hurricane, September 10, 1974
Tagline: Nature's most destructive force unleashed!
Using actual footage from Hurricane Camille, this disaster flick follows the denizens of a Gulf Coast town in the face of a storm's fury. The populace includes Larry Hagman, Martin Milner, Jessica Walter, Barry Sullivan, Michael Learned, Frank Sutton (*Gomer Pyle*'s Sgt. Carter), and Will Geer. Learned and Geer were also working together at the time on *The Waltons*.

Savages, September 11, 1974
Yet another retread of *The Most Dangerous Game*, in which man hunts man using the laws of the jungle. Andy Griffith steps out of his folksy persona to play a killer who needs to snuff his only witness, poor Sam Bottoms.

The Sex Symbol, September 17, 1974
One of the early fictionalized versions of Marilyn Monroe's life—the 1958 stunner *The Goddess*, with Kim Stanley and script by Paddy Chayefsky, was the first and remains the best—had the misfortune of Connie Stevens in the title role of Emmaline Kelly. Stevens is just fine in lighter fare, but she's not up to re-creating the sexy mystique of Monroe. Shelley Winters, an actual friend of Monroe's in real life, and comedian Jack Carter play it straight, but this coarse drama is probably the least worthy of any Monroe biopic, unless you're actually out looking for cheese.

• Don Murray plays a thinly veiled composite of John and Bobby Kennedy, both of whom were rumored to have had affairs with Monroe. Murray co-starred with Monroe in *Bus Stop*, in which she gave arguably her finest film performance.

• Producer William Castle, known for his prolific and often bizarre stunts to sell his horror films, was typecast as a Hollywood magnate.

The Day the Earth Moved, September 18, 1974

A good cast—Jackie Cooper, Stella Stevens, Cleavon Little, William Windom, and Beverly Garland—populates this disaster movie, an *Earthquake*-lite that predated the big screen treatment (which was a colossal hit two months later). An aerial-photography duo (Little and Cooper) discovers that infrared photography can predict earthquakes, and immediately find one about to hit a small desert community. The disaster scenes were filmed in the ghost town of Dry Lake Nevada, about 30 miles into the desert from Las Vegas.

• Former teen idol Bobby Sherman, moved from acting (see *Skyway to Death*, Season Five) to co-producing with this MOTW. (He also co-composed the score.) *The High Point* (N.C.) *Enterprise* reported that Sherman and his producing partner went to Dry Lake, and convinced a recluse named Clyde Cannon, who lived alone there and owned the few buildings still standing, to allow them to be demolished. Other buildings that were slated to be demolished elsewhere were trucked in and also used for the film.

The Great Niagara, September 24, 1974

Shot at the Canadian-side falls, the story follows a father (Richard Boone) and sons (Michael Sacks and Randy Quaid) who guide and rescue those interested in conquering Niagara Falls in 1934. The *Albuquerque Tribune* picked this MOTW as its "Best Bet" for the night it aired, and raved, "*The Great Niagara* is an extraordinary, powerful film excellent in all respects: writing (a fine script by Robert E. Thompson); acting (Boone, Sacks, Quaid, and Jennifer Salt are all marvelous); music (a memorable score by Peter Link); [and] William Hale's direction. The film has the gripping inevitability of a Greek tragedy and is not to be missed. ... [it] beautifully recreates the Depression era, which forced men into desperate [acts]."

The California Kid, September 25, 1974

This was the MOTW series' 200th film. ABC publicity noted of the plot, "After seven speeders have deliberately been sent to their deaths by a psychotic sheriff, the brother of a recent victim rolls into town in a powerful hot rod and forces the lawman into a final high-speed duel." It might sound clichéd, but with young Martin Sheen playing the James Dean role, scary Vic Morrow as the sheriff, and some rippin' car-chase scenes, the movie packs a surprising wallop. Michelle Phillips is wasted as Maggie, a disposable love interest.

• The California Kid is not Sheen's nickname in the movie; it's the name of his "hot rod," a souped-up 1934 Ford coupe.

• Joe Estevez, Sheen's younger, look-alike brother and uncle to Charlie Sheen and Emilio Estevez, has a small role in this film

• Nick Nolte had two MOTW roles, both minor, on his way to TV and movie fame. *The California Kid* was his first, *Death Sentence* (see next page) his second.

The Stranger Within, October 1, 1974

Barbara Eden plays a woman who is abducted, after which she finds herself pregnant. It soon becomes obvious to her that her unborn child is controlling her weird behavior. Could it be the child is otherworldly? This is, essentially, *Rosemary's E.T. Baby*, and you'll either roll with it as Eden downs unbelievable quantities of salt, scalding-hot coffee, and raw meat, or you'll be laughing so hard it won't matter.

Death Sentence, October 2, 1974
Adultery has been a favorite Hollywood theme since the advent of film, and the MOTW was no exception. This time, Don Davies (played by Laurence Luckinbill) is married (to Susan, played by MOTW fave Cloris Leachman), but having an affair with John Healy's wife (Healy is played by a young Nick Nolte, and it's a small part). When Healy's wife is murdered, Nolte is fingered by the police, but Leachman becomes a juror on his trial and begins to suspect someone else: her husband! Leachman, looking pained and earnest in every scene, adds to her quota of wives-in-jeopardy roles with this courtroom melodrama.

Where Have All the People Gone?, October 8, 1974
They've been turned to white dust by a freak solar flare-up … except for a small group of survivors, who band together to figure out what happened and stay alive. Peter Graves, as an archeologist, and Kathleen Quinlan head the cast.
• 1984's *Night of the Comet* was a similarly themed big-screen cult movie, though the situation was played more for laughs. A comet passes close to the earth and leaves everyone who is outside either a pile of red dust or a future zombie. The world, in this case, is saved by a couple of Valley Girl sisters (Catherine Mary Stewart and Kelli Maroney) and a pre-*Star Trek: Voyager* Robert Beltran.

Hit Lady, October 8, 1974
In which the teleplay would have us believe a beautiful young thing (popular personality of the time Yvette Mimieux) is an "elegant, cultured, professional artist" who moonlights as an

assassin. She can't quit, you see. This is mainly an excuse for gorgeous Yvette to slink around in designer clothes and the occasional bikini … with fine-looking Dack Rambo as eye candy for the rest of us.

Locusts, October 9, 1974

The title insects threaten crops near a small town in the Midwest. Notable for a high-powered sitcom cast acting all serious, including Ron Howard (pre-*Happy Days*, unless you count the series' 1972 *Love, American Style* pilot), Katherine Helmond (pre-*Soap*) as his mom, and Lisa Gerritson—about to move from *Mary Tyler Moore* to spin-off *Phyllis*; she played Cloris Leachman's daughter on both sitcoms—as his sister.

• *Locusts* flashes us back to the mid-1950s insects-on-a-rampage horror flicks like *Them* and *Beginning of the End*. And we never get tired of the genre: a TV movie also called *Locusts* aired In 2005. In the latter film, the bugs were bio-engineered.

Bad Ronald, October 23, 1974

Tagline: The Wood family doesn't know it. But the old house they've just bought is already occupied … by a psychopathic killer.

Buzz Kulik directed one of my favorite MOTWs, from Lorimar, the folks who brought you *The Waltons*. When 15-year-old Ronald (the perfectly creepy Scott Jacoby) accidentally kills a teen neighbor who was tormenting him, his panicked mother (Academy Award winner Kim Hunter, picking up a paycheck) decides to create a secret room adjacent to one of the bathrooms of their house to hide Ronald and keep him from harm. Trouble is, she dies during an operation, and Ronald's still living there when a new family moves in. *Uh, oh!* Ronald has drilled holes so he can spy on everyone in the house, and has retreated into a fantasy world where he's the "prince" who must rescue the "princess" from danger. Of course, the family has three pretty daughters who are perfect fodder for Ronald's fantasies. A young Dabney Coleman played it straight as the father of the family who moved in; Lisa Eilbacher (*Beverly Hills Cop*, *An Officer and a Gentleman*) and her sister Cindy were two of the daughters. Aneta Corsaut, who played Andy Griffith's Mayberry gal-pal on *The Andy Griffith Show*, also had a small role.

• A French version of this movie was made in 1992 (*Méchant Garçon*, which translates as *Naughty Boy*).

• According to the online All Movie Guide, "In the original John Holbrook Vance novel on which this TV-movie is based, Ronald abducts, repeatedly rapes and ultimately kills two women." Nothing quite so horrible happened in this MOTW (come on, it was 1970s TV), but it's scary enough nonetheless.

• Though Jacoby was nearing the end of his teen career at the age of 18, he had several younger brothers follow him into acting, including Billy Jayne (Jacoby), whose career blossomed in the eighties when he co-starred on the cult Fox series *Parker Lewis Can't Lose* (1990-'93), playing a teen while well into his 20s. Scott made a handful of movies (mostly horror) and TV appearances in the eighties (including several as Bea Arthur's son on *The Golden Girls*) and later dabbled in directing.

The Mark of Zorro, October 29, 1974

When Frank Langella wasn't playing Dracula onstage, he took parts like this, a remake of the Zorro legend from 20th Century Fox. Part fop and part hero, Langella acquits himself nicely, with the fabulous Yvonne DeCarlo and Gilbert Roland as his folks, Ricardo Montalban as the baddie, and Anne Archer as his sweetie. The series would have followed our swashbuckling hero as he trounced villains with his fancy swordwork.

Death Cruise, October 30, 1974

Kind of a low-rent rip-off of *Murder on the Orient Express*, set on a boat. Several couples are invited on a cruise, not knowing they're really being set up for ... murder! But the cast is fun and it's tightly woven by producer Aaron Spelling. Ship's doctor Michael Constantine (*Room 222*) tries to figure out the connection between the passengers in the hope it'll help him solve the murders. Richard Long, Polly Bergen, Kate Jackson, Edward Albert, and Celeste Holm are all aboard.

The Great Ice Rip-Off, November 6, 1974

Ice as in diamonds, not skating. Director Dan Curtis left his more familiar horror playground to helm this cute caper. A quartet of jewel thieves—mastermind Gig Young and accomplices Robert Walden (*Lou Grant*), Matt Clark and Geoffrey Lewis—take their $4 million in diamond booty on a bus from heist to heist (Young picks up each accomplice at the next bus stop, where they pull the heist). Little do they know a retired detective (Lee J. Cobb) is also on board. Grayson Hall, who starred as a number of characters on Curtis' cult gothic soap opera, *Dark Shadows*, plays Cobb's wife.

All the Kind Strangers, November 12, 1974

The press release notes, "Seven strange orphans with eight vicious dogs turn a remote farmhouse into a prison for unsuspecting travelers who will either become their parents or disappear permanently." Stacy Keach is the latest unsuspecting traveler to stumble on this odd "family," who happens to be holding "mom" Samantha Eggar (obviously too young to be all the childrens' mother) hostage. Keach is dependent on the kids' vote as to whether he lives (and stays as "dad") or dies. Co-stars Robby Benson and John Savage went on to better-known work. Shot on location in Lebanon, Tennessee.

The Gun, November 13, 1974
The NRA wouldn't like this movie, one of several from Hollywood that take a weapon, in this case a .38-caliber revolver, and follow its "life" from creation through various owners. A no-star docudrama approach accents the plot to great effect, touching on such ahead-of-its-time issues as kids and mentally disturbed people having easy access to a deadly weapon. Director John Badham would helm one more MOTW (*The Godchild*, opposite page) and then have his first theatrical hit, 1976's *The Bingo Long Traveling All-Stars & Motor Kings* (oh … and go on to direct *Saturday Night Fever*, *WarGames*, and *Short Circuit*, among others).

It Couldn't Happen to a Nicer Guy, November 19, 1974
Okay, this must have been a first: a comedy that deals with male rape. ABC said, "Being abandoned on the highway without his clothes is the first of the hilarious consequences faced by a mild-mannered husband who has just been violated at gunpoint by a gorgeous woman." I suppose the fact that no one will believe him, or, if they do, wonder why he's complaining, is even more hilarious. Don't worry, this gem will never be seen again—the Politically Correct Police will assure that. Paul Sorvino is the hapless "victim," and Michael Learned his wife.

Panic on the 5:22, November 20, 1974
The 5:22 is a commuter train, and the passengers panic because bad people are trying to hijack it. Former pro footballer Bernie Casey and *Mission: Impossible*'s Lynda Day George are among

those trapped in the clichés. Rent *The Taking of Pelham One Two Three* instead, a theatrical release about a hijacked subway train that offers true suspense and tension, which beat this MOTW to the punch by opening October 2, 1974.

The Godchild, November 26, 1974

A remake of the 1948 John Wayne classic *3 Godfathers* (both were based on a story by Peter B. Kyne, both made by MGM), in which three outlaws come upon a dying woman and her baby in the desert, and agree to raise the child. A slight change makes these fellows—Jack Palance, Jack Warden, and Keith Carradine—Civil War-era POWs fleeing the Confederates and the Apaches. In any case, when in doubt, go for the John Ford-directed classic.

Betrayal, December 3, 1974

This thriller is lifted by its two leads: Amanda Blake (in her first role following the long-running TV Western, *Gunsmoke*) plays a lonely widow who hires a young female companion (Tisha Sterling), unaware—there'd be no plot if she was aware—that the girl and her boyfriend (played by Sam Groom) are planning to take her money and then (gulp!) murder her.

• Blake was very happy to be leaving the Wild West and her role as saloonkeeper Miss Kitty. Less than three weeks after announcing her retirement from *Gunsmoke*, Blake, "began her starring role in *Betrayal*," reported the Lumberton, North Carolina, *Robesonian*. "'I was delighted to be offered the role,' said the beautiful redhead. 'You may not believe it, but it's my first dramatic role outside of *Gunsmoke* in 19 years, and it's a contemporary story, too. I'm finally out from in front of that bustle and from under a few yards of crinoline at long last. You have no idea what it feels like to wear modern-day

clothes. Do you blame me for being excited over the role?'"
Jeez, no wonder Dennis Weaver left before the series' end.

Only with Married Men, December 4, 1974
A routine stab at comedy, this silly MOTW wastes a game
cast—including Michelle Lee, David Birney, John Astin, Judy
Carne, Dom Deluise, and Gavin MacLeod. The plot, such as
it is: Lee, burned by single men, decides to date only married
men; Birney pretends he's married in order to date her. Fill in
the blanks here.
• Lee returned to this topic in a drama, the 1989 TV movie
Single Women, Married Men, in which she starred as a woman
who forms a therapy group for single gals involved with
married men. Based, according to UPI's Vernon Scott, "on the
true accounts of a female family counselor in San Diego, who
held get-togethers with other single women carrying on affairs
with married men. They want to be needed and loved and
have some sort of relationship. … Lee said the TV film is not a
condemnation of single women who fall in love with married
men. Neither does it necessarily approve their choices."

Roll, Freddy, Roll, December 17, 1974
A literally rollicking comedy: Computer programmer Tim
Conway tries to become an expert skater in order to impress
his son by earning a place in the *Guinness Book of World Records*
(by living on roller skates for seven days). Conway's ex, played
by Ruta Lee, has remarried a famous local guy named Big Sid
(Jan Murray), who stars in his own TV commercials. If your
idea of fun is Conway as a pallbearer on skates, this is the
movie for you. Conway did all his own stunts in the movie.
He told the Port Arthur, Texas, *News* that, "It's pretty hard to
get hurt taking a spill if you know what you're doing."

Let's Switch!, January 7, 1975

Two of my favorite Barbaras, Eden and Feldon, play former college friends, now a housewife and a trendy magazine editor, respectively, who decide to switch lifestyles in this still-relevant comedy. The chemistry between the two leads is fabulous, and who could resist the "Agent 99 meets Jeannie" factor?

The Missing Are Deadly, January 8, 1975

Ed Nelson and Leonard Nimoy topline this (potential) disaster flick: "A rat, infected with an incurable virus that can kill a hundred million people in three weeks, has been taken from a lab by an emotionally disturbed teenager, who disappears, causing a city to panic as more and more people develop symptoms of the disease," reported the ABC publicity machine. The kid was, of course, just trying to get attention from his cold-fish scientist dad. Featuring Marjorie Lord (*The Danny Thomas Show*) and Kathleen Quinlan.

Satan's Triangle, January 14, 1975

The title location is more familiarly known as The Bermuda Triangle. It's where Kim Novak (the sole survivor of a shipwreck) and her would-be Coast Guard rescuers (Doug McClure and Michael Conrad) find it's not cool to mess with the devil … especially on his turf. Add *The Flying Nun*'s Alejandro Rey as a priest Novak and her doomed husband (*Dallas*' Jim Davis) rescue while out fishing, a few clever plot twists, and decent acting from the cast … and you've got a tingly little thriller. No spoilers, but I will say this: not everyone is who they appear to be.

The Hatfields and the McCoys, January 15, 1975

A retelling of the famous family feud (set in 1800s Kentucky) offers a solid Western cast, including Jack Palance, Steve Forrest, Richard Hatch, James Keach, and Robert Carradine.
• Sci-fi fans fondly remember Hatch for his role as Apollo on the series *Battlestar Galactica* (1978–'79). He also lent his voice to the *Galactica* video game and appeared (as a different character) on the updated Sci Fi Channel version of the show (2004–'08).

The Abduction of Saint Anne, January 21, 1975

If you combined *Hart to Hart*, *The Godfather*, and *Joan of Arc*, you might get this movie, in which Robert Wagner is a detective who, along with Bishop E.G. Marshall, tries to extricate a 17-year-old miracle worker (Anne, played by Kathleen Quinlan) trapped in her father's house. The problem: her dad's also a godfather … the kind that runs the Mob … and has "friends" who want to keep his daughter imprisoned.

The Trial of Chaplain Jensen, February 11, 1975

Military law, pre-*JAG*: Handsome chaplain James Franciscus is accused of having an adulterous affair with vixen Lynda Day George, and is the first clergyman ever court-martialed for committing adultery, as a result. Based on a true story, Jensen was ultimately acquitted by the military court—he contended that the two wives in question made advances to him on the pretext of discussing their sex lives with him—and went on to write a tell-all book that exposed the adulterous goings on (including wife-swapping) among officers and chaplains alike in Navy bases such as San Diego and Long Beach, California.

A Cry for Help, February 12, 1975
The title cry comes from a suicidal girl to a cynical, trouble-making talk-radio host (Robert Culp) who mishandles the call, then feels guilty and tries to find the young woman, enlisting his listeners to help, before it's too late!

The Family Nobody Wanted, February 19, 1975
James Olson is a minister, Shirley Jones his wife, and together they take in more kids than the Bradys and Partridges combined. This was a remake of a well reviewed 1956 *Playhouse 90* presentation that starred Lew Ayres and Nanette Fabray. Both treatments were based on the book by Helen Doss. Doss and her husband Carl adopted 12 racially mixed children, kids that nobody wanted and who were considered "unadoptable," in the years following World War II. The book was a best seller, in its 24th printing at the time of this MOTW. Doss, who was the "technical advisor" for this MOTW, told the *Kokomo* (Indiana) *Tribune* on February 15, 1975, that, "This story is mainly a quiet drama of love. It covers a period of several months in our lives in 1947 when bigotry and misunderstanding nearly drove us away from a small town where Carl had come to take over the ministry in a local church." Shirley Jones asked Doss on the set if she felt it was worth all the trouble, and Doss replied, "I honestly never gave it a thought. And after getting to know the dozen youngsters playing her children in the film, I'd like to start all over again by adopting these kids."

You Lie So Deep, My Love, February 25, 1975
Ironside's Don Galloway and Barbara Anderson leave Raymond Burr behind to tackle this thriller in which they're married: He's got a mistress and wants her money, she's a wealthy prig (who, for example, worries about a taxi fare costing too

much). All Galloway wants is Anderson's money … and his mistress. Walter Pidgeon (playing Anderson's uncle) and Russell Johnson give good support. Not the greatest suspense movie ever made, but the chemistry between Galloway and Anderson (who acted together on *Ironside* for four years) makes it worthwhile. And it's one of my favorite MOTW titles.

• Johnson is forever identified with his role as the Professor on *Gilligan's Island*, though he's got hundreds of TV and film credits (stretching back to 1953's *Adventures of Superman*).

Someone I Touched, February 26, 1975

No, not as in "by an angel," but rather, someone touched by VD. Ewwwwww! This icky plot has husband James Olson— going from minister to cad within a week; see February 16—cheating on wife Cloris Leachman, who gets not only an STD but pregnant as well. Talk about your mixed blessings…. This was the end of Cloris' varied husband problems (for the moment)—it was her final MOTW role.

Trilogy of Terror (a.k.a. *Tales of Terror*), March 4, 1975

Directed by Dan Curtis and written by horror master Richard Matheson (as was *Duel*; see Season Three), and based on his short story "Prey." Curtis was the man behind the cult, gothic soap opera *Dark Shadows* (1966-'71), and he brought that same sense of menace to this trilogy of short films, each with a dark theme, and each starring Karen Black. In the first, she played a teacher with a student who has a major crush on her. In the second she plays two roles, a good sister and a bad sister. But it's the third segment, "Prey," that makes this movie a classic: Karen gets a scary-looking, pint-size Zuni fetish doll that, it turns out, is inhabited by an evil spirit. This spirit wants to get out of the doll and into a person. The result is a tense, sometimes violent, and always mesmerizing battle between woman and doll. The final shot of the film has always haunted me. Featuring Gregory Harrison (*Trapper John, M.D.*), George Gaynes (the *Police Academy* movies); and John Karlen (from *Dark Shadows* and later of *Cagney & Lacey*).

Karen Black tries to figure out the motivation behind the behavior of her co-star, a Zuni fetish doll, on the set of *Trilogy of Terror*. This film, and specifically this segment of the film, is perhaps the best-recalled MOTW of the entire series. Dan Curtis Productions

• Made way before the advent of digital graphics, the herky-jerky stop-motion effects, punctuated by horrible-sounding low growls, add to the scares, rather than detract from them. That and Black's emotional, compelling performance will keep you awake at night.

• In the first segment of the film, "Julie," Black plays a drab college professor who is inexplicably hit on by the hot Robert Burton. At one point, Burton (as Chad) takes his "crush" to a drive-in flick. The movie playing is director Curtis' other MOTW masterpiece, *The Night Stalker* (see Season Three).

• The original Zuni doll was housed at Curtis' Santa Monica, California, production offices for many years, until he passed away in March 2006. According to his associate, Jim Pierson, there were multiple Zuni dolls used in both the 1975 original and the 1996 sequel; Curtis had kept one from each movie. In the fall of 2004, Majestic Studios, in conjunction with ABC-TV Consumer Products, released a maquette (statue) of the Zuni Fetish Warrior Doll, based on photographs of the original taken "from every angle to make an exact likeness," according to Majestic CEO Rick Phares.

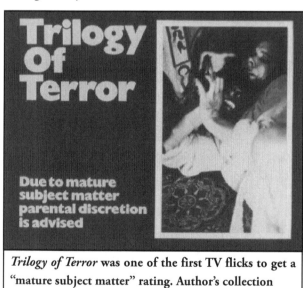

Trilogy of Terror was one of the first TV flicks to get a "mature subject matter" rating. Author's collection

• Prolific (more than 200 films) sci-fi, horror, and fantasy writer/producer/director Charles Band has said that his cult series about strangely alive often-deadly puppets (1989's *The Puppet Master* and its eight sequels as of this writing) was inspired by the Zuni doll in *Terror*.

• *Trilogy of Terror* was remade (for the USA cable network) as *Trilogy of Terror II*, by original director Curtis; it aired on October 30, 1996, with Lysette Anthony taking over for Karen Black. The only story kept for the 90-minute remake was "Prey." Though reviews of the remake were respectable, I can't imagine anything topping the genuine horror of the original Zuni segment. Anthony also appeared in Curtis' resurrection of *Dark Shadows*, in January 1991, as Angelique.

• The original Zuni title, "Prey," was changed to "He Who Kills" in the remake. "He Who Kills" is the name of the warrior spirit animating the doll in the original (as attested to by a scroll that came with the doll).

• In summer 2006, a Zuni doll replica was shown in an episode of the miniseries *Nightmares and Dreamscapes*, in a story about toy soldiers that come to life and exact revenge on a hit man.

• On August 29, 2006, a special edition DVD of T*rilogy of Terror* was released, featuring commentary from Karen Black and writer William F. Nolan plus two short films — *Richard Matheson: Terror Scribe* and *Three Colors Black*.

The Desperate Miles, March 5, 1975

To show that the handicapped are handi-capable, Vietnam vet Tony Musante (as Jim Mayo) decides to make a lengthy trip using his wheelchair. Here's the ABC publicity: "A grueling 130-mile trip in a wheelchair holds unexpected dangers for a Vietnam amputee veteran, who continues his trip knowing it will cost him the woman he loves and possibly even his life [threatened by a disturbed trucker he encounters during the trip].” In real life, the trip was more rewarding and less dramatic: Bob MacKenzie of the *Oakland Tribune* talked to the real Jim Mayo the night the film aired. Mayo, who stepped on a land mine at Chu Lai in Vietnam and lost a leg, noted he made the trip to “prove that people can do just about anything they make up their minds to do. You’ve got to think positive. … The VA gave me a decent wheelchair, one of their better ones, so I decided to see how far I could go. I started out at Long Beach, California, and headed along the coast. No, it wasn’t a motorized wheelchair. I made about 20 miles a day, sometimes more. I ended up in Balboa Park, 113 miles in eight days. I couldn’t believe all the attention I got … the way people would meet me along the way, thanking me for getting out and doing it.” Mayo served as technical adviser for the MOTW and occasionally doubled for Musante.

• The movie was filmed along the Pacific Coast Highway, on the streets of Los Angeles and Long Beach, and on the sets and back lot of Universal in 11 days. Musante (who’d added an odometer to the wheelchair he used) traveled a total of 36.7 miles on it.

Huckleberry Finn, March 25, 1975

Or, *Happy Days Does the Classics*, starring Ron Howard as the title character and classical actor Donny Most as Tom Sawyer! With the erstwhile Huggy Bear (see *Starsky & Hutch*, April 30), Antonio Fargas, reigning it in as a more subdued Jim. And featuring Tom Bosley in drag as advice-giving Aunt Polly … *gotcha*!

Dead Man on the Run, April 2, 1975

Working Title: *New Orleans Force*

Peter Graves was TV’s go-to guy when producers needed solid but unspectacular acting in a drama, suspense, or spy thriller.

After five years on *Mission: Impossible*, Graves teamed up with a producer/director team from the long-running *Hawaii Five-O* for this unsold pilot. Here, he portrays the head of a special strike force, that's part of the Department of Justice, who uncovers an assassination plot. Except for the government involvement, it sounds an awful lot like *M.I.* It took place in New Orleans and would've been set there had it gone to series, because, Graves told Bob Thomas of the Associated Press, "The networks have explored the cities that are appealing on television. New York has been done. Also San Francisco and Los Angeles. Jack Lord has Honolulu locked up. That left New Orleans." O-kay. (Never mind Boston, Philly, Baltimore, Atlanta, Dallas, Sante Fe, Las Vegas, Chicago, Phoenix, San Diego, and so many others....) To my knowledge, there has yet to be a long-running TV series set in New Orleans (though the sitcom *Frank's Place*, starring Tim Reid, gave it an awful nice try for 22 episodes in 1987-'88).

*Returning Home, April 29, 1975

It's obvious why, in the Vietnam era, a production company would remake a World War II movie about three returning soldiers re-adjusting to life at home—the parallels make it very relatable to a new audience. *And* they wanted to turn it into a series. But when the original film is a bona fide classic (1946's *The Best Years of Our Lives*) and can still relate on its own, why bother? Maybe the Samuel Goldwyn Co. (which produced the original and this retread) had nothing better to do. Dabney Coleman and Tom Selleck head the cast of this error in judgment.

• As in the original Academy-Award winner, the handicapped soldier (played in 1946 by the twice-Oscared Harold Russell, who lost both arms in World War II) was played by a disabled veteran (of the Vietnam War, this time), James Miller.

* *Starsky & Hutch*, April 30, 1975

This was the 90-minute pilot for the series starring David Soul and Paul Michael Glaser (two hot guys in tight jeans for the price of one!). The series took off the following fall; it lasted four seasons (1975-'79) and 93 episodes. In the pilot, a young couple is murdered in their car, and it turns out the intended victims were Starsky and Hutch. Memorable co-star Antonio Fargas, a tall, skinny caricature, was the quintessential 1970s bar owner/street playa-pimp/informant, Huggy Bear, decked out in wild platform shoes and furs. He became a series favorite and seventies icon.

• Director Barry Shear, who also helmed episodes of the series, was an experienced, reliable director who had such shows as *Police Woman, Get Christie Love!, Alias Smith and Jones, S.W.A.T., McCloud*, and *The Streets of San Francisco* on his résumé.

• Glaser and Soul both cameo'd in the big-screen update of the series (2004). Ben Stiller and Owen Wilson took over the roles of Starsky and Hutch, respectively, and played the script for homoerotic laughs, among other inside jabs at the series.

*Matt Helm, *May 7, 1975*

Slick Tony Franciosa took over for Dean Martin (the big-screen Helm) in the TV version of Dino's tongue-in-cheek spy thrillers. Helm had given up spying and become a private dick. This pilot for the one-season TV series (1975–'76) co-stars Laraine Stephens, also in the series.

* *The First 36 Hours of Dr. Durant*, May 13, 1975

There's nothing here we hadn't already been seeing on a weekly basis since 1961, when Ben Casey and Dr. Kildare kicked off their five-year runs. Or since 1969, for that matter, when *Marcus Welby, M.D.* and *Medical Center* hit the air for seven years each ... which is probably why this pilot never

made it. A young doctor (Scott Hylands) who's a bit too much of an idealist is thrown into the soup—making life or death decisions!—on his first job. Oh, the drama! Oh, the déjà-vu!
• Hylands played a doctor again in another unsold pilot, 1976's *Angel's Nest*, which ran as an episode of *Medical Center*.

Promise Him Anything, May 14, 1975

The final MOTW of the series was a romantic comedy about a computer dating service and what a man does when his date reneges on the "anything goes" vow she made on her computer card: He sues her. With Eddie Albert, Frederic Forrest, and Meg Foster, who should have sued for improper use of talent.
• Albert, who co-starred in one other MOTW, *See the Man Run* (December 11, 1971), was already appearing in the detective show *Switch*. Best known as would-be farmer Oliver Douglas on the sitcom *Green Acres*, he said, in an interview the day this MOTW aired, "working with and watching these youngsters [Forrest, Foster, and Steven Keats] took me back to my own days as an actor," when he was a contract player at Warner Bros. in the 1930s. "Their enthusiasm, their lighthearted horseplay between scenes, reminded me of our fun in making films." The "our" Albert referred to included his contemporaries Wayne Morris, Ronald Reagan, Jane Wyman, and the Lane sisters, Priscilla, Rosemary, and Lola. Albert plays Forrest's free-spirited dad in the movie, and he noted that, with the computer angle, the MOTW was an update on "the timeless blind date situation. Had the film been made 35 years ago, it would have had Priscilla Lane playing Meg's part, Wayne Morris in Steve's role, and I would have been cast as the shy guy Fred plays. Who would have played my role? Why, who else but Alan Hale?" [Hale was the look-alike father of *Gilligan's Island* Skipper Alan Hale Jr.] Albert, who died at the age of 99 in 2005, said one of the perks of working in TV was the chance to act with young, up-and-coming actors.

Afterword

With several notable exceptions (including *Trilogy of Terror* and *Starsky & Hutch*), *The ABC Movie of the Week* had peaked before its final season (1974–'75). The films were telling stories that were mostly retreads (or downright implausible) by the end of its run. This partly accounts for the fact that neither the Tuesday nor Wednesday movie made the Nielsen Top 30 in its final year as a series.

Since theatrical movies were also becoming more accessible to TV, the "movie of the week" concept didn't seem as new and wonderful as it did when the series debuted six years earlier. Still, it was a healthy run, longer than many sitcoms or dramas, and its legacy can be felt today mostly on cable stations, like the USA Network, WTBS, and Sci Fi Channel, all of which produce their own movies.

Like the MOTWs, some of these are good, some are bad, and some are so bad they're laugh-out-loud funny. The best of the MOTW legacy is perhaps most keenly seen today on pay-cable channels like Showtime and HBO, both of which produce original movies (with few restrictions on topics, sex, and language, so they can deal with pretty much any subject) like *Angels In America*, *Dirty War*, *My House in*

Umbria (all HBO), and *Good Fences* and *Bang Bang, You're Dead* (Showtime).

These films, by tackling normally verboten subject matter like drug abuse, gun violence, racial inequality, AIDS, the outcome of germ warfare, aging gracefully, and more, continue the *Movie of the Week*'s own sterling track record in dealing with similar subjects. We can only hope that the MOTW classics not yet available on DVD will be recognized as such, and released (imagine a double feature of *Brian's Song* and *The Sheriff*, or *Trilogy of Terror* and *The Screaming Woman*; some might even be able to manage extras like director and star commentaries, and, dare we hope, deleted scenes).

There are probably too many rights issues preventing the entire series from being released on DVD. But that doesn't mean you should stop looking. That's exactly the reason eBay and the Internet were created. And when you're not searching, try writing to the producers or production companies that made these classics, if they're still around, and telling them you would buy new releases.

I know lots of fans would welcome these films back into our living rooms.

Appendix

A note on those dates that fit the MOTW schedule in March through May of 1975 (Tuesday or Wednesday nights) but for which I could not find films in the first edition: On these dates, ABC either aired MOTW repeats or preempted the MOTW for special programming. See below.

March 11, 1975: A repeat of *Killer Bees* (originally aired February 26, 1974)

March 12, 1975: A repeat of *Scream of the Wolf* (originally aired January 16, 1974)

March 18, 1975: A repeat of *Ordeal* (originally aired October 30, 1973)

March 19, 1975: MOTW preempted for the special *Jane Goodall and the World of Animal Behavior: The Hyena Story* (in Tanzania's Ngorongoro Crater; narrated by Hal Holbrook)

March 26, 1975: A repeat of *The Girl Most Likely to...* (originally aired November 6, 1973)

April 1, 1975: A repeat of *Savages* (originally aired September 11, 1974)

April 8, 1975: A repeat of *Guess Who's Been Sleeping in My Bed?* (originally aired October 31, 1973)

April 9, 1975: A repeat of *The Story of Pretty Boy Floyd* (originally aired May 7, 1974)

April 15, 1975: ABC aired a movie special in place of the MOTW, Irwin Allen's remake of *Swiss Family Robinson*, a two-hour pilot starring Martin Milner and Pat Delaney as the parents of the shipwrecked family, and a very young Helen Hunt. It became a 20-episode series in the 1975-'76 season, with most of the same cast, plus Frank Langella as Jean LaFitte.

April 16, 1975: A repeat of *The Bait* (originally aired March 13, 1973)

April 22, 1975: The MOTW was preempted for a repeat of ABC's blockbuster, Emmy-nominated miniseries, *QB VII*. It originally aired in April 1974 in two parts, but ABC reran it in three parts. The miniseries—which centered on a Nazi war-crimes trial and is generally regarded as one of the best ever produced—was nominated for 13 Emmys and won six.

April 23, 1975: The MOTW was preempted for a repeat of Part Two of *QB VII* (see above).

May 6, 1975: A repeat of *The California Kid* (originally aired September 25, 1974)

Regarding *The Deadly Game*, which aired September 25, 1971, a Saturday: I could find no further information on this movie, though it was listed in a 1974 self-congratulatory ad celebrating 200 ABC Movies of the Week.

As for *Smile When You Say "I Do"*—also mentioned in the ABC ad, and which I listed as "lost" in the first edition of this book—it aired September 25, 1973, a Tuesday. See the regular listing for details.

Selected Bibliography

Books:

—*The Complete Directory to Prime Time and Network Cable TV Shows, 1946-Present*, Sixth Edition by Tim Brooks and Earle Marsh, October 1995

—*Movies Made for Television: The Telefeature and the Mini-Series, 1964-1979*, Alvin H. Marill, 1980

—*Performer's Television Credits, 1948–2000*, David Inman, 2001

—*Total Television*, Fourth Edition, by Alex McNeil, 1996

—*The TV Guide Film and Video Companion*, Friedman/Fairfax, 2002

—*Unsold Television Pilots, Vol. 1, 1955–1976*, Lee Goldberg, 1990

—*Unsold Television Pilots, Vol. 2, 1977–1989*, Lee Goldberg, 1990

Web sites:

—www.amazon.com

—www.bijouflix.com

—www.bn.com

—www.pro.imdb.com (subscription needed)

—www.revengeismydestiny.com/MadeforTV.html

—www.sitcomboy.com

—www.tvparty.com

About the Author

As a Baby Boomer and child of the television era, *The ABC Movie of the Week* was a special treat for me, satisfying my desire for drama or comedy or horror or science fiction every week, and then twice a week. The series challenged me, entertained me, and fed my love of movies.

I graduated from college with a Masters in Communications, so it seemed only prudent to communicate, and so I did, becoming a magazine writer and editor in New York City. After a quarter-century in publishing, I landed my dream job: as Copy Chief at *Soap Opera Weekly*, I am mandated to watch TV every day!

In 2001, I wrote my first book, focusing on the first TV star to leave a major impression on me via that little box in the living room: Lucille Ball. The widespread acclaim for *Lucy A to Z: The Lucille Ball Encyclopedia*, convinced me there were lots of other Boomers who wanted to read about television, movies, and the celebrities they watched growing up. In January 2008

I published an expanded, revised and updated 4th Edition, with pictures for the first time, many of them exclusive.

I've lately specialized in showbiz topics and interviewed many celebrities, an eclectic list including such Lucille Ball associates as *I Love Lucy* film editor Dann Cahn; Lucy's personal secretary, Wanda Clark; chauffeur Frank Gorey; and Lucy's surviving co-stars Doris Singleton (Carolyn Appleby) and Jane Connell (her *Mame* Gooch); plus Susan Lucci, Johnny "Guitar" Watson, David Hedison, Denise Nickerson, Gale Storm, actors Jason-Shane Scott and Ignacio Serricchio, crooner Phyllis Hyman, and behind-the-scenes movers and shakers like *Wonderfalls* creator Bryan Fuller and *House MD*'s executive producer David Shore.

While copy chief at *Computer Shopper* in the mid 1990s, I began working with my late, talented friend, *Dark Shadows* aficionado and author Craig Hamrick, also a fine photographer (my author's photo is his work), and the result is the book series TV Tidbits. Go to www.sitcomboy.com for more information.

My other books include *Kiss Me, Kill Me*, featuring Craig's atmospheric photos; its prequel, *Sleeps Well With Others* (2006); *Lucy in Print* (2003); my first TV Tidbits book, *Funny Ladies* (2004, redone as *Sitcom Queens: Divas of the Small Screen* in 2006); and, also in 2004, *The Lucille Ball Quiz Book*. *The ABC Movie of the Week Companion* is my third contribution to our ongoing series. My latest was *The TV Tidbits Classic Television Book of Lists*, published in 2007.

I've been an invited guest at various nostalgia conventions—including several Lucy Fests held in her hometown of

Jamestown, New York and sponsored by The Lucille Ball-Desi Arnaz Center — and the Big Apple Con comic and nostalgia conventions, where I've served on author panels, provided insights and trivia as the "celebrity guest" on bus tours of Jamestown, and hosted *I Love Lucy* trivia events.

I've been interviewed on many radio shows, including WCBS-FM New York, the biggest "oldies"/nostalgia station in the country, and KSAV on the Internet, a.k.a. TalkingTelevision.org; quoted and reviewed in various national magazines, from niche market publications like *Classic Images* to mass-market magazines like *Star*; quoted and referenced in other books about Lucille Ball (like Stefan Kanfer's 2003 *Ball of Fire*) and comedy (Lawrence Epstein's 2004 *Mixed Nuts: America's Love Affair with Comedy Teams*); and interviewed for an upcoming documentary about the Lucy fan phenomenon.

I steer clear of Zuni fetish dolls.

Index of Movie Titles